PRISON PRODIGY

POWER, PRISON, & A PURPOSE REBORN

by

Kyle Overmyer
and Natalie June Reilly

Edited by Natalie June Reilly

Written by humans for humans.
No generative artificial intelligence (AI)
was used in the writing of this book.

This book is dedicated to God for loving me and for never leaving my side. You were my rock at the bottom.

*To Mom & Dad, for always loving and supporting me through the hardest times of my life and never turning your back on me.
I love you both!*

To Mikayla & Dillon, my amazing children, for continuing to love me when it hurt the most and for teaching me the true definition of "resilience." I love you both, and I am so proud of you kids!

*To Jennifer, my beautiful wife and best friend, thank you for loving and believing in me when I had absolutely nothing.
You are the missing piece of my puzzle. I love you mucho!*

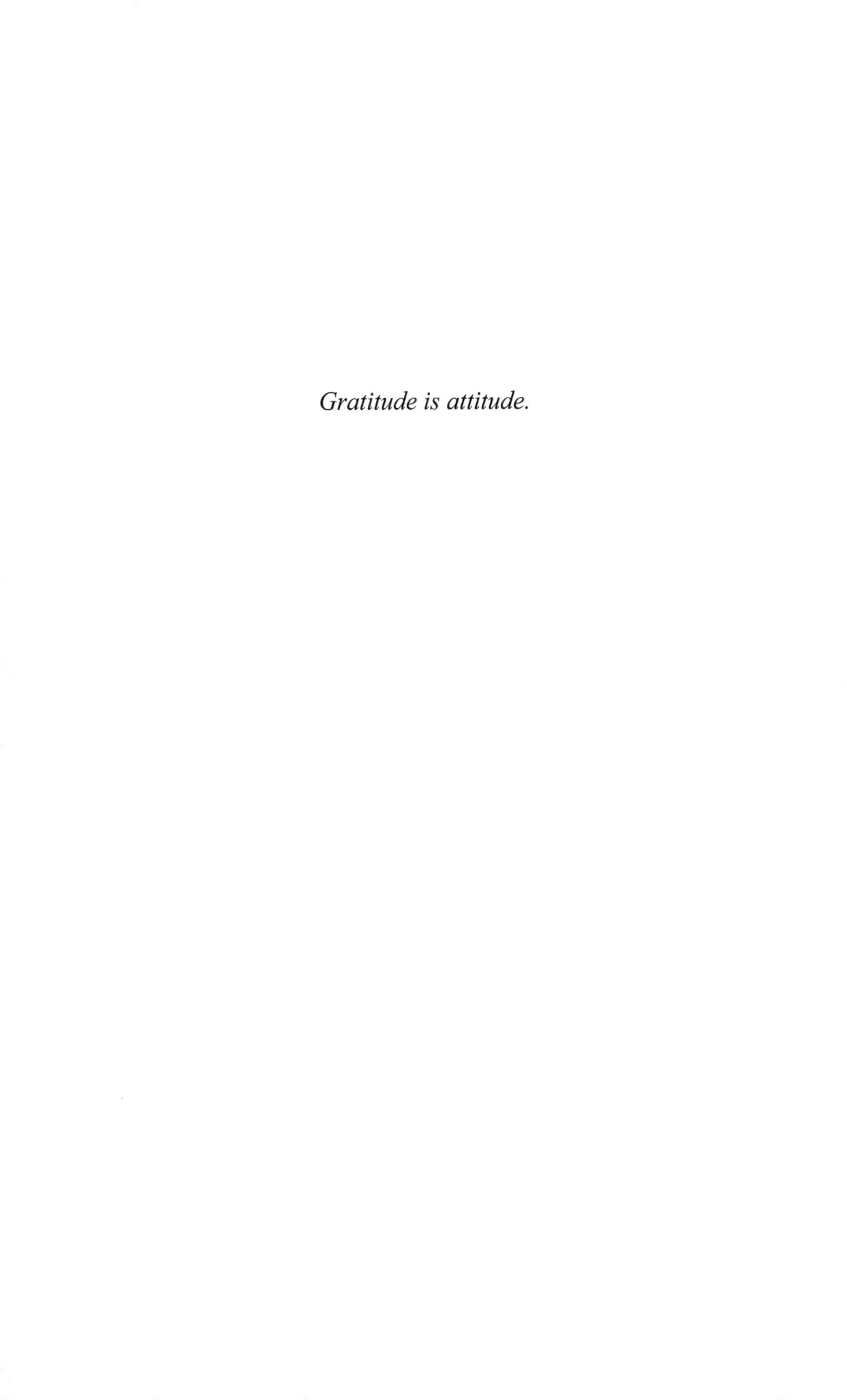

Gratitude is attitude.

TABLE OF CONTENTS

PROLOGUE
SECOND LIFE

own an old pair of black dress shoes that are a bit worn around the edges but are no worse for the wear. I'm not the original owner, and I have no idea the miles they've traveled before me and in what capacity, but I do know the shoes fit my feet comfortably. I've had them for several years now, and if they could talk, they would tell you that I am a man who has made grave mistakes in his life and is on a hard-earned journey toward redemption. Like those secondhand, black, leather soles, I, too, am a bit worn around the edges but no worse for the wear.

This particular pair of shoes has its own story of reclamation and has been given a second life, which, in a way, makes us a good fit to walk on this journey together. Since my release from prison on April 6, 2020, I have been given the gift of a second life. After serving a four-year sentence, I was homeless, divorced, ostracized, and bankrupt—financially, emotionally, and spiritually.

It was ground zero.

To satisfy my parole requirements, I got a job frying chicken in my hometown of Fremont, Ohio, the same town I'd been elected sheriff twelve years earlier. Larry Bowman, a friend of mine who owned a couple of Lee's Famous Recipe Chicken restaurants, took a big chance on hiring me. It meant a lot that he still had my back, especially since the public I once protected and that once revered me was now looking down on me in disgrace.

Folks actually came into the restaurant just to poke fun at me, mocking me while I fried chicken. When I was sheriff, I used to eat at that same restaurant with my deputies. Those same men and women continued to show up for lunch and dinner. They watched me sweat over buckets of "honey-dipped and hand-breaded" raw chicken parts, wearing blue jeans and boots saturated in chicken grease for $9.50 an hour. I became the butt of a really bad joke. It was my own fault, really. My dad always says that when life goes sideways, it's nobody's fault but your own.

He's not wrong.

Social media trolls wasted no time posting cruel memes using my sheriff photo, deliberately having a good laugh at my expense. It was all so surreal, and while it hurt, I knew that I could either give up or turn it up. I decided I was going to let the experience humble and encourage me. I knew that I could make a comeback. I also knew that there were a lot of people who wanted to see me fail, and I was not about to give them the satisfaction. I was going to do everything I could to better myself and be the man I knew I could be. I wasn't sure how I was going to do that, but I was determined to make it happen.

While working for Lee's Famous Recipe Chicken, I applied for other (less greasy) jobs. I knew with a felonious rap sheet it would be a bit of a gamble, but I had to give it a shot. A local clinic reached out and invited me to interview for an administrative job. I had nothing respectable to wear, but I was able to pull together a secondhand suit. The only trouble was that I did not have shoes to go with it.

Lucky for me, a friend of mine who worked at a behavioral center had recently tossed out a few bags of used clothing and shoes into a back-alley dumpster. I can't say it was my finest hour, but I saw an opportunity and dove in after the bags of used duds when no one was looking. I had officially sunk to the level of a dumpster diver. I was in full-blown survival mode. I know that act should have made me feel clever and courageous for being so resourceful, but all it really made me feel was embarrassed. When I was sheriff, I saw numerous homeless people living on the street, digging through other people's garbage. Never in a million years did I think I would be one of them.

While rummaging through the bags of used clothing, I found that used pair of black dress shoes, and they fit me perfectly. They were not in mint condition by any means, but I figured they could be cleaned up and polished enough to serve a purpose.

I mean, who was I to judge?

I, myself, was in a state of repurpose. I wore the secondhand suit and black (dumpster) dress shoes to the job interview. I felt human again, and even though I did not get the job, at least I was making strides in a forward direction. I couldn't go back to my old life, even if I wanted to. I had burned that bridge and everyone on it.

In 2008, at the age of thirty-four, I was the youngest sheriff to be appointed in the state of Ohio, Sandusky County. I was something of a celebrity. Everyone knew and respected my family and me. I was always proud of the fact that people genuinely liked me. I loved my community, and I was proud to serve it. Sandusky was my county.

At the time, I lived in Clyde, just ten minutes outside of the county seat of Fremont. There, the local folks are blue-collar, mostly farmers and factory workers. There is a high population of migrant workers, due in part to the field labor opportunities. Every morning, when I rolled up to work, I could smell tomato paste cooking at the Heinz factory. It was literally in the backyard of the sheriff's office, along with Whirlpool.

Sandusky County is a rural community with a lot of farmland and, unfortunately, a lot of illegal drugs. Being sandwiched between Chicago, Detroit, and Cleveland, the county is a hub for crime and all the problems that go with it. In the 90s, at the start of my career, there was a crackdown on crack cocaine. The sheriff's office conducted a federal drug sweep, executing a series of raids to clean it up. Toward the end of my career, there was a heroin epidemic. Today, it is fentanyl. As sheriff, I was working hard to rid the streets of drugs and crime. What nobody knew was that I, myself, was hooked on prescription pain pills—opioids.

What began as a means to lessen severe arthritis pain became a life-altering dependency. I was masking my pain with the help of prescription pills. At home, I kept them stashed behind my duty weapon, safely tucked away in the laundry room. I trusted my secret was safe because everyone in the house knew not to touch my gun.

I kicked off my morning routine with Vicodin, Percocet, and a giant Polar Pop of Pepsi from the Circle K. That was the cocktail that kept me charged. I took pills throughout the day, up until the late evening. It was all I could do to get through. There were days I took up to twenty pills. Over the course of two years as Sandusky's sheriff, I was prescribed more than a thousand pills. I lied to myself and to others about it. I was desperate to numb the pain and forget about everything, starting with the struggles of the job. I saw a lot of death in my career, including three drownings, all of whom were children. I didn't pull the trigger, but our department was involved in a fatal shooting. I had a hard time with that, too. Everything was catching up to me—financial and marital issues and being sued as sheriff for millions of dollars.

The irony: I was always good about getting the brave men and women in my department the help *they* needed, but when it came to taking care of myself, I let it slide. I was the sheriff of the county. I was supposed to have a big "S" sewn on my chest. I was a tough guy, made of Teflon. Instead of dealing with my issues, I held all of my pain, anger, and hurt inside. In my mind, it was shameful to ask for help. The truth is, I hated myself. I did not like the man I had become.

On the outside, I wore a Kool-Aid smile, but on the inside, I was probably one of the saddest people you would ever meet. I was a good actor, one of the greats, because not even the people closest to me knew I was falling apart. I was dying inside. And yet I was fully functional. It was crazy!

I carried pills in the chest pocket of my uniform. I would randomly pop a few when I "needed" them, like just before giving a speech. When my supply ran low, I counted the days until it was time for a refill. If my supply got really low, I cut the pills in half just to keep from feeling "the sickness" that seeped in when I ran out.

Those pills owned me.

I was an unhappy man—at home, at work, and in my own skin. My addiction turned me into a liar, a cheat, and a master manipulator. I was engaging in an extramarital affair, as if the addiction wasn't bad enough. I had to find other ways of coping with the pain. I was relentlessly running from reality, and I was quickly running out of steam. Eventually, I decided to stop taking the pills and, for the most part, I got myself clean. While the physical addiction was no longer a problem (or so I thought), and I was convinced that the whole dilemma had gone away when I flushed the last of my stash down the toilet, I was still struggling—mentally, physically, emotionally, and spiritually. I was far from out of the woods.

In December of 2015, while running for reelection, an investigation was opened. My fishy prescription patterns had been red-flagged by the pharmacy, and an Ohio Automated RX Reporting System (OARRS) report was run on me, tracking the "dispensing and personal furnishing of controlled prescription drugs."

It was determined that I had been "doctor shopping" for opiate prescriptions for some time. Not only that, but I was stealing from my dad's prescriptions and from the take-back box at the sheriff's office. The truth was out.

On August 23, 2016, the day the grand jury was to meet, I was still in denial. I was never going to admit that I was an addict. In fact, I was convinced that I would *not* be indicted. I mean, I was the sheriff, the big "**S**" of Sandusky County. I was cleaning the streets of drugs, not getting arrested for them. Besides that, I worked with these county commissioners and judges. I thought for sure I would get through it unscathed, but by 6:30 p.m. that night, following a ribbon-cutting ceremony at the Sandusky County Fair, I was forced to turn myself in. And it still hadn't sunk in! Even while sporting an orange jumpsuit, looking at a forty-three-count indictment and fifteen years in prison, I was telling myself, "I got this!"

The famous last words of an addict.

A small part of me was worried, but my ego was in complete control. I continued to reassure myself. I continued to think, *I can beat this!* I honestly believed I could flush it all away, like I did the pills.

I was wrong.

I plead guilty to obtaining drugs by deception, tampering with records, theft, and theft while in office. Suddenly, I was no longer Sandusky's finest. I was a forty-one-year-old felon looking at a four-year prison sentence. I had failed my family, my friends, and my county. Moreover, I had failed myself.

As a man, I've made a lot of mistakes in my life, beginning with not being honest with myself. Consequently, the extramarital affair cost me my marriage. The addiction and subsequent incarceration cost me my freedom and everything I cared about most in the world, including precious time with my kids, my home, my life, and the public's trust. The entire experience humbled me, and it changed my life forever, which is why I keep those black dress shoes as a reminder of how low my addiction took me and, conversely, how far I've come since.

Those secondhand shoes taught me that with a little resourcefulness, courage, introspection, humility, and shoe polish, I could be a better man—I am redeemable. I am addiction's worthy adversary, deserving of a second life. So many people counted me out, but I never gave up on myself. It was not easy by any stretch. I can honestly say this was, hands down, *the* hardest lesson of my life. And at the same time, this journey has been its own reward.

If I could go back in time, I wouldn't change a damn thing—I would change nothing. I have no regrets in my life. I believe this was all a part of God's divine plan, because even though I am a recovering addict with a felony record, I have since found the missing pieces of my life's puzzle. That wouldn't have happened otherwise. We need the struggles and the failures to achieve greatness. We also need to take accountability, regardless of the outcome. It's never too late to do the right thing!

The good news is, as hard as life can be, we don't have to do it alone. It took me a long time (and a damn hard lesson) to realize that God's purpose for my life was always there. It's there for you, too. Isaiah 41:10 reads: "So do not fear, for I am with you; do not be dismayed, for I am your God. I will strengthen you and help you; I will uphold you with my righteous right hand."[1]

---

[1] *The Bible*, Isaiah 41:10 New International Version

All this to say, the moment we give our life to God and take responsibility for our actions, life naturally gets better—maybe not at first, but eventually. Most of my life, I was just so afraid to ask for help. Fear got in my way—fear of disappointing people, fear of disapproval, and fear of failure. And then there was the deepening insecurity and sadness that came from never having heard the words "I love you" from the one man I needed to hear them from the most.

God's purpose for my life began long before I was elected Sheriff of Sandusky County. I can't help but believe the road has always been leading to this, and it's because of that difficult patch of pavement that I can say with certainty that **no one is beyond redemption**. I am living proof of that. With God's grace and a little grit and gumption, we all have it in us to make a strong comeback. It's not always pretty, but it is possible. A used pair of black dress shoes and a man who died on the cross for my sins reminded me that there is hope for us all. That was never more evident than on the day I married the most beautiful woman (my best friend!) wearing those same black dress shoes. But I'll tell you all about her and that day a little later. In the meantime, I invite you to take a walk with me.

ONE

SMOKEY'S SON

I was the youngest of two children. I grew up in a two-parent household. I attended a private Catholic school from the fourth grade through my high school graduation, and I was always smaller than the rest of the kids in my class—short and pretty thin. I played football and made it

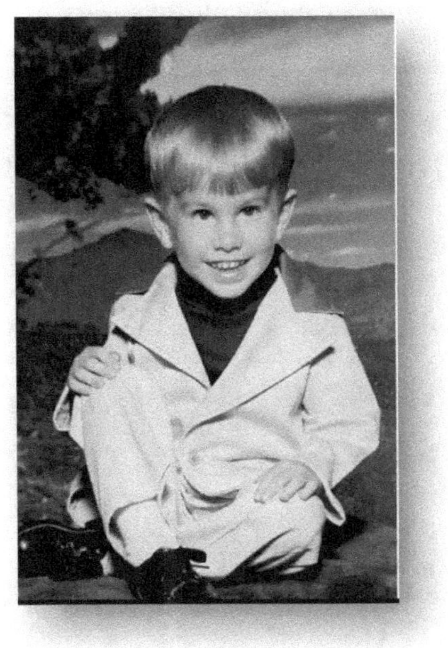

onto the wrestling team for Fremont St. Joseph's Central Catholic High School. I even boxed for a short time during my freshman year. I was all of one hundred and twelve pounds (soaking wet!) and not even remotely muscular. My slightness in stature, however, did not stop me from playing sports and continuing to work out with weights in the big, white barn behind our house, with my dad's name painted on the broad side: P.A. Overmyer—short for Paul Arden. It was a pretty standard rural upbringing, just east of idyllic.

People who knew my dad on a personal basis called him Smokey. He was well-respected in our community, a deputy who, after more than thirty years, retired as a captain. Everybody wanted Smokey to run for sheriff, but he never did. Dad made a good living. He provided well for our family. Every couple of years, he would trade in his pickup truck for a new one, paying the difference in cash. He kept a big toolbox in the bed of that truck, with the words "Smokey Overmyer—Lindsey, Ohio" painted on the side.

Dad instilled in me a strong work ethic. He always put food on the table, clothes on our backs, and a roof over our heads. I remember him saying, "It's not a disgrace to be poor; it's an inconvenience." That always stuck. My dad was old school. He was a coon hunter who made extra money selling coon hides door to door. It was his side hustle. Back then, the locals in Lindsey ate coon meat. So, he sold that, too. When I was working as a deputy, I remember making an arrest and seeing my dad, who was off duty at the time, walking into the house next door. He was hustling coon in the hood, making a delivery. There I was, making arrests, and Dad was delivering someone's dinner. He worked hard. I never forgot that.

Growing up, I lacked confidence. I always felt super insecure. I think it had much to do with my perceived feelings of how my dad felt about me. I'm not sure he ever quite "got" me. In fact, he used to tell my mother, "Kyle can be *your* project."

That always hurt more than I let on.

No matter how much time and energy I put into sports and school, I just never felt good enough in my dad's eyes. I really had a hard time believing in myself because of it. I tried desperately to feign confidence, but I got stuck in the lack of love I felt from Smokey. I never could get past it. That lack of confidence caused me to be less aggressive and unassertive in terms of accomplishing any goals I may have had growing up. Looking back, I think the thing I wanted to achieve more than anything was my dad's love and approval. I wanted to show him that I could do and be more than he ever thought was possible. And I wanted to hear him say those four allusive words: "I love you, son."

I believe there is a difference between having a dream and a vision. Where dreams are make-believe—temporary—visions are seeing what you want to achieve and going for it; they are true to who *you* are, as much as they are a passageway to your ultimate destination. Do people ever truly arrive at *that* destination? I don't think we do. I don't think we live long enough, but we come close.

Most people underestimate their true potential and what they can achieve. I know I did, and it didn't help that my dad doubted me even more than I doubted myself. He never encouraged me to go to college. He felt it would be better if I graduated from high school and went to work at a local factory. He definitely wanted me to stay away from a career in law enforcement. I remember him saying, "It's just not worth the headache, and it's not for you."

Growing up, I was terminally bored and needed to escape country life as often as I could. There were no other children to play with or relate to as a kid. When I wasn't playing whiffle ball in the yard, I was spending a lot of time alone—sketching. I loved to sketch! If I am being honest, art was my first true love. Not a day went by that I wouldn't find myself sitting at the kitchen table drawing pictures. Being an artist and something of a dreamer, I was naturally closer to my mom than my dad. Sketching was actually a good way for me to cope with the fact that Dad and I couldn't really relate to one another.

We lived out in the sticks, in a small village in Sandusky County called Lindsey, Ohio. It is the halfway point between Cleveland and Detroit. The winters are cold, and the summers are warm and humid. The people are also warm and always willing to lend a hand in times of need. Of course, living in a rural area, we had animals. With animals came chores. I, myself, had four donkeys—Daisy, Dandelion, Dalia, and Daffodil. I shoveled a lot of shit in my youth. On the weekends, I was expected to wake up early in the morning and work the land. Dad worked the day shift as a law enforcement officer, so there was always a long list of chores that instilled in me as much value and responsibility as they did work ethic. Although it didn't allow much time for being a kid.

When I was fifteen, I would spend weekends at the house of a close friend of mine, a guy who lived in the city of Fremont. His parents would often go out of town, giving us the run of the place. When that happened, we would write our own rules. With the help of his older brother, my friend and I would throw big parties and experiment with alcohol. I had discovered a newfound freedom!

I remember paying some older guys in the neighborhood, who were legally old enough to drink, to buy us alcohol. Being so young and not very big in stature, it didn't take much to get me intoxicated. I quickly came to realize that every time I drank too much, I fixated on my insecurities and the fact that I never felt "good enough."

On one occasion, the alcohol overtook me, and I poured my soul out to a friend. I expressed my deepest, darkest hurt and the experience of never feeling worthy in my dad's eyes. I literally broke into tears, which made me feel even worse because crying was a sign of weakness.

I never saw my dad cry, and to this day, he's never said those three little words that every kid needs to hear, and it made me question everything, including his true feelings for me. I wondered, did I not measure up to his standards as a son? Did he wish he had never had me? And if so, why? There were so many unanswered questions. I struggled every day with that, and I carried that heavy feeling with me everywhere I went, like an anchor. I'm not trying to make excuses for having fallen prey to addiction, but I believe my perception of my relationship with my dad (or lack thereof) held me back for a long time.

After graduating from high school, I enrolled at the University of Toledo as an art major. I took the majority of my classes at the Toledo Museum of Art. Not only did the program allow me to grow as a person, but it also helped me find myself. I changed my appearance for a short period of time, dressing more progressively. I let my hair grow long and pierced both my ears.

When I went home for the holidays, my dad elected to drive to Toledo to pick me up. I did not own a car, so more often than not, I bummed rides from family and friends. Otherwise, I took the bus. It had been several months since I had seen my family. So, to avoid any heavy discussions about the length of my hair, I stuffed it into a Seattle Seahawks ballcap. Firstly, I was a huge Brian "The Boz" Bosworth fan. Secondly, I was hoping to conceal my long, wavy mop. It was a moot point, however, because I forgot to take out my earrings. Needless to say, my dad was totally against men having long hair and earrings—pierced or otherwise.

As I lumbered into the passenger side of his Ford pickup truck, my dad immediately did a double-take. Judging by the grimace on his face, the earrings made him angry.

"Take them out," he barked.

Well, hello to you, too.

I did as he asked without hesitation.

"Take off the hat," he said.

No hug. No hello—just do as I say!

I exhaled as I removed the hat from my head. My long, wavy hair dropped like a theatre curtain over my shoulders, blanketing my eyes and neck. The sight made him even angrier. He grumbled, "We will be stopping to get you a haircut on the way home."

True to his word, we stopped off at the local barber. The hair I spent months growing out, one of the first acts of my adult independence, became a casualty of coming home. I felt as though my true identity had been stripped away because of this man who, for whatever reason, never fully accepted me. I was just starting to figure out who I, Kyle Overmyer, was for the first time in my life. And he squelched it before I even made it home. Seriously, why did he even care? I wasn't *his* project.

From that point forward, I began to focus on the "new" me. If I wasn't going to be tall, I wanted to be strong. This had everything to do with my own sense of masculinity. I saved up my money and invested in a weight bench and a variety of weights. I really wanted to bulk up, put on size. I was inspired by bodybuilders like Arnold Schwarzenegger and Lee Haney. I had a vision of myself having a physique like those guys, hoping it would give me the confidence I needed to accomplish more in my life and to, perhaps, change my dad's opinion of me. I thought if I could put on muscle and weight, everything else would work itself out. What I did not realize at the time was that a boy growing up without a strong emotional connection to his father struggles to know his own self-worth. I could see other young men around me, aiming to make their dads proud, and it was working. It just wasn't working for me. So, I fixated on my body image and outward strength, thinking that would solve everything.

While still enrolled at the University of Toledo, I met new friends who were also into bodybuilding and looking their best. I became so obsessed that I began to experiment with anabolic steroids, synthetic hormones that promote growth and repair muscle tissue. At the time, they were readily  accessible in the gym. A lot of people were using them. The man I was beginning to see in the mirror was how I had envisioned myself all my life, especially as a young boy. I began competing in powerlifting. This was just another way for me to show my dad that I was strong. I didn't want him to think I was weak—inside or out. I wanted to be admired. I don't think it was narcissism so much as human nature, a young man seeking validation from his father. My sense of self-worth was fragile. However, my physical strength was surging. I was strong for my weight class. At my first few benches and several after, I took first place in powerlifting. I was dominating!

I eventually started training at Gold's Gym in Toledo, Ohio. I began to connect with people who were more into bodybuilding than I was, and some of them were even competing professionally. It inspired me to get even more aesthetic and lean. Not only was it more appealing to me, personally, but it was also attracting the attention of women.

After my sophomore year in college, living and breathing the gym and the party scene, I decided to drop out of the University of Toledo and move back home. Honestly, I was born with a small-town mentality, and it kept me from moving too far from what I knew. My aspirations, however, were bigger than my small-town mindset. So, I saved my money and paid cash for my first car. I was working odd jobs—the local gym and different factory jobs, including Crown Battery, where I worked the midnight shift, pouring hot lead and nursing the resulting burns. I was still trying to figure out what I wanted to do with my life. I considered becoming a professional bodybuilder and moving to California, but that was only a pipe dream, temporary, not the vision I had for my life.

I had to figure out who and what I was outside of the gym and the factory. I went to my dad and asked for his advice, particularly in relation to a career in law enforcement. I figured he had made a go of it—putting a roof over his family's head and food in their belly. Not only that, but he was well-respected in the community. Again, he insisted I work a "normal" job and stay away from law enforcement. But did I listen?

Heck no!

What stubborn, young, self-respecting son listens to his dad?

In 1995, I pulled some money together and enrolled in the local police academy in Fremont. I continued to live at home with my parents, lifting weights in the barn. My mom always had my back, but I still struggled to gain acceptance from my dad.

In the spring of 1996, I graduated from the police academy. My mom and dad were both in attendance. Encouragingly, my dad was the one to hand me my Peace Officer Training Academy certificate when my name was called. That was cool, a real honor. In a way, it was like a father passing the torch to his son, and with it came a feeling of acceptance. Without words, it felt as though he was saying, "I am proud of you, and I love you, son!"

It was something I will never forget, something to build upon, even though I knew he didn't want me to be a law enforcement officer. Was he proud of me? I don't know, but I like to believe he was. The truth is, I was happy and proud of myself, and that was affirmation enough for the vision I had for my life.

TWO
SANDUSKY COUNTY'S YOUNGEST

I was barely twenty-one years old when I started working corrections at the sheriff's office on Cinco de Mayo in 1996. Three years later, I married my first wife. I really didn't know what I wanted to do with my life. It was while working in the jail that I learned a lot about the inmates coming in and out, understanding how the streets and judicial system worked, to say nothing of human nature. I was jonesing to be out on the streets, fighting crime on the frontline. So, what did I do? I became a road patrol officer for the Sandusky County Sheriff's Office.

I loved it!

It was the late 90s, and the crack cocaine epidemic had blown up, taking our small, rural town by storm. It bothered me that the streets had become chaotic and violent. I excelled in drug interdiction. For some strange reason, *that* was my niche—traffic stops, taking drugs, money, and guns off the street. It made me feel like I was doing something good for my community. It makes me emotional just writing about it.

Those were good times!

My wife (at the time) was a schoolteacher and highly educated. She encouraged me to go back to college. I always knew that I wanted to do more than just settle into an average career in law enforcement. So, I went back to school and obtained an associate degree in criminal justice from Terra State Community College in Fremont, Ohio.

Our first child, Mikayla, was born eleven days before our first wedding anniversary. She was an "oops" baby, but the best kind of oops! Our son, Dillon, came along in 2003, around the same time I obtained a bachelor's degree in business administration at Tiffin University. It would be the same university my son (and future wife,

Jennifer) would graduate from years later.

It's interesting how life comes full circle.

With two degrees in hand, one in each fist, I became laser-focused. I started working hard, attending lots of training, and excelling in the workplace. I eventually got appointed to our SWAT team, graduating from the FBI SWAT academy. It was great preparation to do more! I met a lot of people, including some great FBI agents who started pursuing me to come over to the federal side as an agent. My wife encouraged me to apply, so I did. I was educated and good at my job, so why not?! I even interviewed with the Secret Service once or twice.

In 2003, one week before our son, Dillon, was born, I received a call from Sandusky County Sheriff David Gangwer. He wanted to meet for lunch. I thought I was in trouble because, knowing how busy this guy was, I never wanted him to have to make time to see me.

"I want to talk to you," he said.

Oh shit!

So, we met for lunch at the Golden Dragon. It was the local hot spot for law enforcement officers. We routinely met there. Sheriff Gangwer sat down and shot right from the hip. He said, "Hey, I hear you are thinking about leaving the sheriff's office."

"Yup," I replied. "I want to better my future for my family. I feel like I can do more than what I'm doing now."

"Well, you're doing a hell of a job," he exclaimed.

"I'm in love with law enforcement, sir," I said, smiling.

"You have made quite an impact in a short time," Sheriff Gangwer replied. "You are a quick learner, and you kind of remind me of me at that age. I was the same way!"

We both laughed. I still had no idea where this conversation was going, although I got the feeling I wasn't in trouble.

That was a huge relief!

There was a brief silence as the waiter set down two glasses of ice water on the table. Sheriff Gangwer grinned and said, "So, I have an opening in the detective bureau. Are you interested?"

"Well ..." I began. "I just put in for the Feds."

"I'll tell you what," he interjected. "I'll sweeten the pie."

I couldn't believe what was happening. I was sitting across the table from a man (a decorated law enforcement officer) who had been the Sheriff since 1985. He was elected to the position of Sheriff of Sandusky County, serving six terms, making him the longest-running Sheriff in the county. And he was offering *me* a position.

"I'll make you a detective sergeant with rank," he declared.

"Done deal!" I replied without hesitation.

I went home to my wife, and we talked about it. We both figured there would be a chance of having to move all around the country with a federal job, so I became a detective sergeant in Sandusky County. From there, I was on fire! I quickly partnered with the Ohio Bureau of Criminal Investigation (BCI), the Drug Enforcement Administration (DEA), and the Fremont Police Department. Together, over the course of one year, we took over one hundred drug dealers off the street. We boarded up and seized houses, cars, and businesses. I was shutting down the criminal element.

Sheriff Gangwer came back to me around Christmas time and said, "I want to talk to you."

Again, we sat down for a chat over mu shu chicken.

"Merry Christmas," he smiled. "I am making you Captain!"

In that conversation, I became one of the youngest detective captains in the history of Ohio. I was under thirty years old, and nothing was going to stop me! I handled homicides, double homicides, and suicides. I was a jack of all trades. Eventually, I performed my first undercover stint in a large-scale theft ring involving over $300,000 worth of four-wheel Kubota tractors. These were big-ticket items. Our town got hit hard! We had no idea what was going on.

One day, while on patrol (plain clothes), I pulled over a dude who had a felony warrant. When I threatened to arrest him, he said, "Hey! I think you might want to talk to me and make this go away."

In other words, he had some information to exchange for his charges and warrants. He had a role within the organization that was involved in stealing these tractors at night. He admitted that he did it to feed his drug addiction.

To make a long story short, he decided to cooperate. That's when I went undercover and joined the theft ring under the guise of a guy named Burt. I went on a series of late-night escapades with these folks, who ended up being well-educated businessmen. Some of them were in the Union. Believe it or not, some of them were boiler workers. They would scout out the items during the day and send their basic flunky out at night to lift the tractors. I became one of those flunkies.

It got to the point where we decided to wrap up the sting. My informant and I were delivering a log splitter over in Ottawa County in Oak Harbor, Ohio, when law enforcement swept in as planned and arrested the lot of us, including myself and my informant. That was the plan. I'll never forget when it was time to go to court. I appeared in plain clothes, and the ringleader walked up to me.

"Hey, Burt!" He exclaimed. "How are you doing?"

"I'm Detective Captain Kyle Overmyer," I replied with a grin.

"I think I need to make a deal," he said.

The ringleader went off to prison, and I kept kicking in doors, taking drugs and dealers off the streets, writing search warrants, taking on small undercover roles, and loving every minute of it! I was out buying $40 worth of crack rocks, making big sweeps of some of the small-time dealers. We were working our way up to the big fish.

One day, I came across a Hispanic individual who had possession of a large amount of cocaine. Lo and behold! He was connected to the drug cartel. He was looking at doing a lot of time. Realizing that this was too big a case for us to handle on our own, I called the DEA. The informant asked for an undercover officer, and because the DEA guy looked like a cop, I became Scottie Pitts for a few years during that investigation. We would order multiple kilos of cocaine directly from Mexico. Someone would pick it up and drive it through Texas all the way up to Fremont, Ohio.

To set up the deal, I would rent a storage unit, where the Hispanic informant and I would wait for the seller to arrive with the multiple kilos of cocaine. As soon as he'd get there, we'd roll down the storage door and break it down. The seller gave me about a week to pay for the product, half a million dollars.

We repeated this exchange a few times before picking him off and tracking him to another state. That interaction turned into a big-ass drug bust! It was headlined in the papers! We made multiple million-dollar seizures. There were guns *and* drugs.

It was great!

Sheriff Gangwer loved it! And he loved me for making it happen. He said, "You've got a real future here. Would you ever consider running for Sheriff someday?"

"I'm pretty young," I replied.

"I'm going to show you the ropes," he said, smiling. "I'm going to groom you."

Not long after that conversation, I was appointed to the Republican Central Committee in Sandusky County, along with other organizations that included one that was dealing with organized crime down in Columbus, Ohio. I remember traveling there with the Sheriff. We'd stop off at a deli in Waldo, Ohio, and eat bologna sandwiches with onion and wash them down with Dr. Pepper.

I recently went back to that place to reminisce. It brought back so many good memories and conversations with Sheriff Gangwer. He was like a second father. He imparted a lot of wisdom to me.

"You're gonna be my guy," he said on a Wednesday, as we headed to a meeting. I'll never forget that day. I was stunned.

"Hey, just remember," he continued. "If anything happens to me, I want you to run for Sheriff."

Wait! What just happened?!

That day, we showed up at our meeting and went about our

business. The very next Sunday morning, I got a call telling me that Sheriff Gangwer had passed away. It came as a complete surprise. He was in his sixties and in great shape. It was a terrible loss for the entire county and for me, personally. I was one of the pallbearers at the Sheriff's funeral.

Soon after, I was approached to be his replacement for an emergency appointment. I talked it over with my wife, and she left it to me to decide. It was kind of a gamble because I could have easily been pushed out the door by the chief deputy, a buddy of mine who had more than thirty years of experience. He had thrown his hat into the ring for the position.

The way I looked at it ... this was business. It wasn't personal. The Republican Party Central Committee voted, and I won unanimously. It shocked the whole county!

I was thirty-four years old. I was officially the youngest Sheriff in the State of Ohio and in all Sandusky County history. I knew I had some big shoes to fill. Sheriff Gangwer looked like a sheriff and was well-respected. I, on the other hand, did not look like a sheriff—

not even close. But I was Sheriff, and I knew that that's what *he* wanted me to be. So, in 2008, there was a new Sheriff in town.

Sorry, I couldn't resist!

I'll never forget the night I was appointed. My dad said, "Kyle, you've got more balls than I ever had."

Coming from Smokey, that felt pretty damn good!

THREE
KOOL-AID SMILE

Everything was going well in the beginning. I will never forget my swearing-in ceremony. I've never seen the courtroom so packed with people. It was wall-to-wall. My wife and children were there to hold the Bible. Folks were sad about Sheriff

Photo Credit: Ken Dumminger

Gangwer's passing, but they were happy to see me step in because they knew what I was all about. I was always in the headlines for seizing drugs. I was a nice guy, but people knew that I meant business. Even the streets were talking. They, too, were happy because they assumed the new position would take me off the streets and keep me from making busts. Little did they know, I planned to be a working sheriff. I was a sheepdog, not a politician! I still wanted to be in the game. That's what made me different. I still patrolled the streets. I rode with my midnight guys and my day guys. I went out with the DEA and the U.S. Marshals to make sweeps. I wasn't your normal sheriff. I was driven! I was still a young man who had a lot of piss and vinegar in him. I had something to prove—to myself and to Smokey.

In 2008, the market was crashing, and people were foreclosing on their homes. Consequently, our budget had been cut by $250,000, so I had to be creative. To save money, I had this idea to create a two-acre sustainable garden inside the fences of the jail. The inmates would grow it and, essentially, feed off it. The community loved the idea and donated all the plant and vegetable seeds. This saved us a lot of money that first year, and it gave the inmates a deepening sense of purpose and appreciation for the food being served.

The next year, I went a step further and had the inmates raise eighty broiler chickens, in addition to growing their own vegetables. This was a tremendous opportunity for them to take pride in their work and the nourishment they were providing for themselves and others. I was feeling pretty inspired at that point, and so I thought of yet another way we could utilize the garden to grow empathy in our inmates.

In Clyde, Ohio, there was a mysterious rash of pediatric cancer. The Ohio Health Department referred to it as the Eastern Sandusky County Childhood Cancer Cluster. It impacted at least thirty-five children between the years of 1996 and 2010.[2] I decided to use our garden to grow a Pediatric Cancer Pumpkin Patch. It was the first of its kind! I thought it was important for prisoners to understand the difference they could make in people's lives. Many of them had never done any kind of community service. It was interesting to talk with them when they were growing the pumpkins. They took pride in

---

[2] Seewer, John, "Mysterious cases of cancer in Ohio children puzzle parents and investigators," Lubbock Avalanche-Journal, December 30, 2010, Clyde, Ohio

what they were doing. Not only was this project saving money, but it was also rehabilitating inmates. Things were going great!

One day, while on vacation with my wife and kids, my ankles started hurting. I could barely stand the pain. When we got home, I went to the doctor and, at thirty-six years old, was diagnosed with arthritis. It was likely caused by years of playing sports, breaking both ankles, and enduring multiple injuries as a kid. I walked away from that appointment with a prescription for one hundred Vicodin. I didn't think much of it. It was all good—for a while.

Life was moving fast. As sheriff, I was winning. I was a recipient of the "20 Under 40" award, where a local nonprofit showcased twenty leaders—all under the age of forty—who had distinguished themselves throughout Northwest Ohio and Southeast Michigan. I received a Chamber of Commerce award and other accolades for the work I was doing.

Life was good!

Then one Sunday, after returning home with my family from Florida, I received a call from my dispatch—a man with a shotgun was threatening to kill his family, and he wasn't going down without a fight. My wife and kids were within earshot of that phone call, and I'll never forget my daughter, Mikayla, saying, "Dad, that doesn't sound good."

"I got this!" I exclaimed.

Those were my famous last words when shit was about to go down. The truth is, I wasn't worried. Me and my department knew what we were doing. We negotiated with this man on the telephone for several hours, trying to get him to come out of the house and surrender. Nothing was working. So, I told my guys it was time to go in and safely take care of the situation.

"I'm going in with you," I added.

I would never send my deputies into a situation that I, myself, wasn't prepared to go into.

We threw a flashbang and stormed the place. The man jumped up off the couch and aimed a shotgun at us. We were forced to draw our weapons and take his life. The family, who called 911, asking for help, immediately turned on us. They said the man was sleeping when SWAT stormed in and shot him. It was a real circus. Two of my deputies and I, along with the Sandusky County Board of Commissioners, were named in a $20 million lawsuit. I was deposed for nine hours straight. It was exhausting. The case went all the way up to the Grand Jury to determine if it was a clean shooting. Ultimately, the evidence pointed to suicide by cop. We won, but it was extremely stressful.

The family protested twice, marching up and down our street. It made the front page of the paper, basically saying that this man's blood was on *my* hands. The thought of that has never left me. The stress took its toll on my deputies, too. I was diligent when it came to getting them the help they needed. I made sure they had all the tools and resources they could get their hands on to take care of themselves. I just didn't do it for myself.

Did the stress of the situation bother me? You bet it did. My drive to get things done started waning. I didn't realize it at the time, but I was falling into a depression. It was a real struggle. It was trauma, compounded by all the autopsies, dead children, homicides, shootings, and close calls. I was carrying the burden *and* the blame.

To make matters worse, I received another call on another Sunday. I don't know what it was about Sundays. I was at my son's basketball game. I was told that three boys, ages seven, eight, and ten, had fallen through the ice in the mouth of the Sandusky River. I rushed out there. I boarded an airboat, but it was too late. The rescue mission turned into a recovery mission. All three boys were dead. They drowned. We pulled them out of the icy, cold water—two brothers and their friend.

The weight of that call was bearing down on me, but I did nothing to help myself. Again, I made sure my deputies were taken care of, but as for me, in my mind, I was too strong—too tough! I was the sheriff, but I was becoming something else. The people around me couldn't see it, but I was dying on the inside. I hated getting up in the morning. I hated living with the pain—physically, emotionally, and mentally. The pills were my friend—they took care of the pain for me. They took care of it all so that I didn't have to deal with any of it— the demands of my marriage, the job, my life. The problem was that my monthly Vicodin prescription of a hundred pills was only lasting a week. I ate a handful of them every day. I was getting desperate. I had to feed the need. I had to kill the pain. So, I started doctor shopping. I went from doctor to doctor, even manipulating the doctor in my own jail. I soon graduated to Percocet. They were much stronger and worked better.

These pills became a mistress, the true love of my life. I started stealing them from my parents. Both Mom and Dad have arthritis, and I knew what day my dad's Percocet prescription was filled. I volunteered to pick it up for him. I went so far as to carry a stapler in my car, so I could steal from my dad's pill supply. He didn't even notice. He trusted me, and I stole from him.

When my daughter Mikayla got her teeth pulled, I took her painkillers, too. I stole anything I could get my hands on to keep my pain at bay. I stole from the drug take-back box at work. When folks from our community tossed their meds into the locked takeback box, I pretended to clean it out. No one suspected anything. I would barricade my door and dump the pills on the floor in my office. I would rifle through them like a kid does with his Halloween candy.

One day, I found a bottle of one hundred Percocet. I was happy in a sick and sad way. I honestly didn't think I was doing anything wrong. I justified it. After all, they were prescription drugs that were being thrown out, and I had a prescription from my own doctor. I was in complete denial. I walked around with a Kool-Aid smile. I was the best actor in town, running for sheriff every four years. Nobody knew that I began and ended my day with those pills. I couldn't live without them. I was in love with them. It was like a romance. I loved those pills so much. I hid them in plastic baggies in my pockets. I'd pop them while attending different events, including my kids' sporting events. I was physically present and accounted for, but I was mentally checked out. I wasn't really there for my children or my wife, and as time wore on, the strain (and lies) took a wrecking ball to my marriage. I was a bona fide addict. I was empty inside. My life was a black void. I needed to fill that void. And that's when I began to cheat on my wife. Cheating for the first time was hard, but it got easier. I justified my bad behavior because I was empty inside. I was sick. Addiction is a disease, but I didn't understand that at the time. I just continued to justify what I was doing, and the infidelity helped me deal with the pain and the lies. It wasn't love. It was an escape.

On February 3, 2015, a visit to the pharmacy began a chain of events that changed the course of my life and my addiction forever. I stopped in to refill my Vicodin prescription. I always filled them on the third of the month—like clockwork. My pharmacist (and a wonderful human being), Leslie, said, "Hey, I want to talk to you."

I didn't think anything of it. I knew her. I knew all the pharmacists. I knew everybody in that town because I was the sheriff. I honestly thought she wanted to talk to me about criminal activity, people making meth out of Sudafed. That's how deep in denial I had become. Leslie and I stepped to the side counter. She looked me in the eye and said, "You're done."

"What do you mean?" I asked.

"We received an OARRS report, and we can see that you're going to multiple doctors and being prescribed narcotics—opiates."

Before I could respond, she stopped me cold.

"You're done, Kyle. I have to report you and cut you off."

The blood drained from my face. I was scared and angry. I had so many emotions running through me. I was a husband, a father, a sheriff, and a community leader. People looked up to me. Many of them voted for me. They put me into power. In that moment, I knew what I had to do. So, I went home and flushed the last of my Vicodin down the toilet. It was over ... just like that. I said nothing to nobody. Over the next few weeks, I got sick—very sick.

Detox sucks!

When my wife and children went to school in the morning, I'd put on my uniform, make it appear as though I was heading to work. I'd even leave the house. Meanwhile, I would manipulate my schedule. I was the boss. I had that ability. Then, I'd make a giant U-turn and quickly return home, pull my vehicle into the garage, put the door down, and lie sick in bed for hours. This was my routine for weeks.

Over time, I was physically feeling better. Mentally, I was still struggling tremendously. I still wanted to use. The opiates made everything go away: the pain, the arguments with my wife, the headaches of the job, the issues with employees. It even made my financial problems disappear. Without the pills, I had nothing to lean on. I could no longer talk to my wife. I couldn't talk to my kids. I never could talk to my dad about anything. He and I were so different! I could have easily gone to my mom, but I didn't want to hurt her.

I stayed clean. I believed I was in the clear. I still had my girlfriend on the side, and that helped to fill some of the void inside of me. I thought I was in love with her, but I didn't have a clue what it meant to love—not really. I didn't know how to love myself. How could I love anyone else? My relationship with this woman was a tall glass of whiskey, just another way to escape.

Primaries were approaching. My neighbor, a local police chief, decided to run against me in the upcoming election. He was gunning for my job. I couldn't let that happen because my work meant everything to me. I didn't know who I was without it. This police chief went so far as to attack my Twitter account, pointing out that I was following (and being followed by) rappers and porn stars. It was a big fiasco! I tried to blow it off, but the hits kept coming. There were articles written about me in the paper, attempting to badmouth me, and even then, folks in my community would approach me and say that they liked me because I was "a real human being and not some stick in the mud."

When the primary results were revealed, I had more than sixty percent of the votes. It was a relief. I thought, *Phew! Here we go. I'm okay.* And everything, for the most part, was okay. Everything was going well, or so it seemed. I was sure that no one had figured out my dirty little secret.

FOUR
EXPOSED

t was less than a week before the presidential election in
2016—Donald Trump vs Hilary Clinton. I received a phone
call from our county prosecutor. He wasted no time getting
straight to the point. He asked point blank: "Are you using opiates?"

At that point, I had been clean for several months, so I really
didn't sweat the question. I figured the inquiry was done for
procedure's sake, a general follow-up to the report that was made.
This county prosecutor and I had a history of getting along well, so I
felt confident that it would all work out in my favor.

"No," I said. "I can pee in a cup if you need me to."

I half chuckled, as if it was all just a big misunderstanding.

"Well," he replied, sounding a lot more serious than I expected. "There have been complaints filed with the attorney general's office, and it appears as though they're going to look into them."

"Okay," I said, feeling the weight of his words in my chest.

The first thing I did after that phone call was retain an attorney—just in case. There were whispers that agents were nosing around the county, asking questions. I saw their vehicles. It was nerve-wracking, but I went about my business of being Sheriff.

On the first day of the Sandusky County Fair, I was invited to cut the ribbon, kiss babies, and shake hands with constituents, judges, state representatives, and congressmen. I showed up to the event in my sheriff's uniform, and by the end of that same night, I was donning an orange jumpsuit, looking at a forty-three-count indictment and fifteen years in prison. I turned myself in and bonded out for the price tag of $150,000. If I am being honest, it bothered me, but it didn't worry me. I assured my wife and kids that it was just a big misunderstanding. I shrugged it off and said, "They're coming after me. They want my job."

To the shock of everybody, I went back to the business of running for sheriff. I was also running from the fact that I was an addict. The people around me started talking about addiction. Of course, I was in denial. My ego was big, and my arrogance was off the charts. I didn't want anybody to know what I had done. I was ashamed, swimming in so many emotions. All the while, I was participating in debates and marching in parades. People would step off their porches to hug me, offering prayers and promising me their vote. The people of Sandusky County didn't want to believe what they were hearing and reading about me in the paper. I think they felt bad for me and chose to support me. My numbers went through the roof. I was lying to everyone, including myself.

My son's thirteenth birthday was approaching. He asked me for a crossbow. So, I went out and bought him one. A week and a half later, I received a call from my attorney.

"Hey, Kyle! Did you buy a crossbow?" he asked.

"I did," I replied. "I got it for my son's birthday."

"They're filing paperwork to revoke your bond because you bought a dangerous weapon."

Oh, boy! Here we go.

A hearing was scheduled in front of a judge. People were slated to appear and testify against me. That morning, I dropped my son, Dillon, off at school. I'll never forget him looking at me and asking, "Dad, am I going to see you tonight for dinner?"

I looked him in the eye and replied with my famous last words, "**I got this!** Have a great day! I'll see you tonight at dinner."

I showed up at the hearing later that same day, and they got me! They revoked my original bond and locked me up—$250,000 cash bond. I was done—booked into Marion County Jail, a tri-county facility where I would immediately surrender to certain truths and to my addiction. I knew it was time. I couldn't run anymore. I was too tired. That's where I attended my first Alcoholics Anonymous (AA) meeting. I began to write letters to the prosecutor and the judge, asking for leniency. And letters of support were pouring in from the community. I talked to my parents about my addiction, but I didn't admit anything to my kids. I couldn't. I was still talking to my girlfriend at the time, so, as you can imagine, my marriage was still very much in the crosshairs of my ongoing deception.

Meanwhile, I worked with my attorney on a plea, and even though I was no longer using drugs, I knew I needed treatment. Mentally, I was struggling. I needed to get myself right. More than anything, I needed to take responsibility for everything. My wife and children were looking for me to do the right thing.

I returned to court on December 13, 2016. The courtroom was lined wall-to-wall with people. My parents were present. My wife was at home. The media was perched in our front yard, a live feed streaming. This was big news!

Out of the forty-three counts, I pleaded guilty to fifteen. I had officially fallen. I was broken. I turned around to face the people in my community, and I apologized to everybody.

"I'm an addict," I cried. "I need help."

And then I turned to the judge to face the music.

"Mr. Overmyer," she began. "What do you have to say for yourself?"

"I'm responsible for what I did," I replied. "I am addicted to opiates. I'm sorry, and I want to make this right. I'd like to go to treatment and take care of my family—get my life back together."

The courtroom got very quiet. The judge leaned in and began to speak. "What troubles the court is …" she began.

My ears were ringing. I could see the judge addressing me, but I could hear nothing. Every so often, I heard words like "doctor shopping," "drug issue," "position of trust," "personal gain," "criticizing the people who took issue with you," "maligning them in public," and "attempting to destroy reputations."

I heard her speak about the issue of public trust and our law enforcement. She said, "They used their badge as a shield. You used it as a sword."

I broke out into a cold sweat as the judge continued to explain the damage I had caused my community, particularly my fellow law enforcement officers. She made it clear that I had abused my position and stolen from the taxpayers of Sandusky County.

She wasn't wrong.

The judge went on to call me selfish, self-absorbed, and narcissistic. She assured me that I was going to get the best treatment in the state of Ohio, and with that, she sentenced me to four years in prison. I felt my knees buckle.

Oh my god! How am I going to do this?!

It felt like the end, but looking back, it was just the beginning. After I was arraigned, I called home to talk to my wife and kids. My wife said, "I know you got four years ... and I know you have a girlfriend."

And just when I thought I had hit rock bottom, a basement door opened up and swallowed me whole.

"What do you mean?" I asked.

"The media played all your jail phone calls for everyone to hear," she said.

I dug the hole, and the media buried me. That was the last phone call I had with anyone for the next thirty days. I was taken to Grafton, Ohio, for intake. I'll never forget the feeling of getting off the bus with one hundred other prisoners from Cleveland. We were stripped down to a number. I became 692183. I was no longer Kyle Overmyer. I was put into the hole for thirty days—solitary confinement. That's where I spent Christmas. I tried calling my kids, but the call got disconnected. I talked to no one, and the only sound I heard for that entire month was the scraping of concrete when it was time to eat.

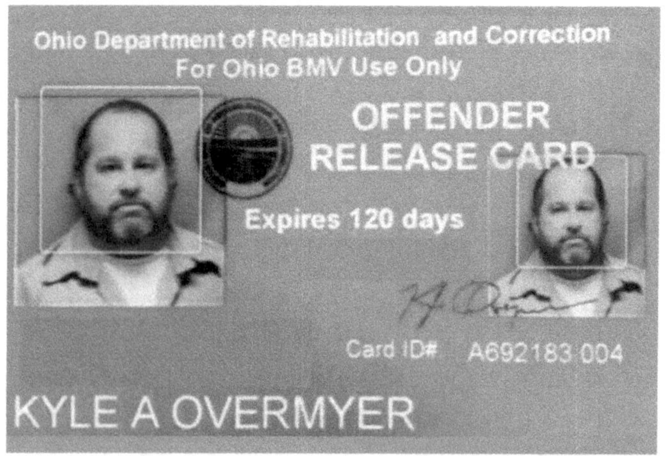

FIVE
692183

eing a prisoner to opioid addiction was far worse than being held prisoner in a penitentiary built from brick, mortar, and barbed wire. I didn't feel half as helpless behind bars as I did chained to those pretty, little pills. In prison, if I felt threatened, I dealt with it the way men do—I fought forward, meaning I took a preemptive strike. With the pills, I was too ashamed to put up even the slightest fight. I made no bold attempts to take matters into my own hands. I just let it slide. Those pills made me weak. Prison made me strong.

My physical and mental strength was developed in "the yard" the prisoner's playground. There, we could enjoy the great outdoors, feel the sunshine on our face and feel somewhere close to our faith and freedom, albeit heavily guarded by two barbed wire fences and large men armed with rifles. We could workout, run, or walk around the track for exercise. Like any playground, fights frequently occurred in the prison yard. There was an unspoken rule: so long as the fight didn't happen in a cell, it was considered a fair fight. And you knew when a battle was about to occur because the crowd moved in a very particular way. Your best bet was to avoid getting caught up in it.

Personally, I enjoyed being in the yard because it was one more way for me to spend some much-needed time alone. Outside, I was able to think about and imagine where I wanted to be after my release. It was good for my mental strength to daydream about life after prison. My cell was small—a bedroom made for two that included a bathroom (with no door) and a bunk mate. It was my place for peace and rest, particularly when my bunkie was away.

The "day room" was a combined living area and kitchen. We inmates shared a microwave, to blow up ramen noodles and heat food, which did not promise a whole lot of flavor. We watched television together in the day room. There were a lot of arguments over what show to watch. The only time everyone agreed was when we watched the news. It was the one thing that made us feel connected to the outside world.

The trip to the commissary was the highlight of our week. We were allowed to order from a short list of foods. The options weren't extravagant, so we had to get creative and plan our meals. And that was only if we were fortunate enough to have money on the books.

Many of the inmates had prison "hustles" so that they could purchase commissary goods. Some inmates made crafts and braided hair, while others painted pictures, shot tattoos, did laundry, and even prostituted themselves. I didn't' have a prison hustle. I was still sort of in a state of disbelief. I mean, drugs and addiction didn't affect guys like me—educated, white, and born into good, intact families. I was an all-American, white, Catholic kid from Ohio.

I grew up to be the man behind the badge, Sheriff Gangwer's understudy. I was at the top of my game and at the pinnacle of my career—drug abuse was other people's problem. I was the guy putting people behind bars for using illegal drugs. How could it be that I was serving time for such an offense? How was it that I was reduced to a number?

Emotionally, I was still struggling—a lot. I had become the worst version of myself—a liar, a cheat, an adulterer, an addict, and now a fifteen-count felon. For me, the hardest part of serving those four years (and coming to terms with my sins) was that I was unable to watch my children grow up. I couldn't look in their eyes and tell them that I loved them and that I was sorry for fucking up! How could I ever explain to them the reasons why I wasn't there to love and protect them like a father should love and protect his children?

I was dealing with my demons, struggling with what I'd seen and done on the job—having taken people's lives and seeing people's lives being taken. I could control the physical pain of my arthritis with the opiates. It was the mental anguish I couldn't conquer, and it caught up with me—fast. I couldn't live without the pills. My demons were too demanding. I had to manipulate them, feed them constantly—first thing in the morning, throughout the day, and before I went to bed at night. Addiction is a disease, but it's not like cancer or diabetes. Addiction distorts reality, tears apart relationships, and devours one's own sense of relief. One day, I had control over all of Sandusky County—the next I was in lockup with zero control. The truth is, even as sheriff, I had very little control. I remember on the third of every month, when it came time to refill my Vicodin prescription, I promised myself that I would quit. "I'm done!" I'd exclaim. "This is the last time I get a refill."

However, by the time the third of the month rolled around, when it was time to quit taking the pills, I was back at the pharmacy— and not just for my own pills but for my parents'. You see, they too suffered from arthritis, and when I wasn't stealing their pain meds from their home, I was volunteering to pick them up from the pharmacy. I'm sure my dad was thinking, "What a great guy my son is, for picking up my prescription."

I loathed myself for it! And that loathing only grew stronger with each passing day. Again, the pills made me weak. Prison made me strong. I think it must have been God's plan all along—to get me alone behind bars, where there was nowhere to go but inward. I had nowhere else to run but to Him.

SIX
FATHER'S DAY

n those four years spent in the penitentiary, I missed seeing my daughter go to prom, graduate from high school, and begin her college career at the University of Toledo. I missed seeing my son play high school varsity sports, and I wasn't there to teach him how to shave. As a father, I missed out on so much. As a man, I own that. I am responsible for stealing those precious moments away, not just from myself but from my kids. Even before I went to prison, I was less focused on making memories with Mikayla and Dillon and hyper focused on burying the shame I felt inside.

My first Father's Day behind bars hit hard. I always celebrated that day with my children. I was struggling not seeing them. I could do the four years in prison, but it was tough not being physically present for Mikayla and Dillon—unable to hold them, hug them, see their faces, and tell them how much I loved them. And it had nothing to do with my ex-wife. She didn't keep them from me. Even though I hurt her in the worst possible way, she was great! My kids just didn't want to see me in that capacity, and I understood that. Not only did they have to deal with me going to prison, but they had to come to terms with me leading a double life. It was awful, and it ended in divorce and bankruptcy. I talked to my kids daily over the prison phone system, and I emailed them when I could, but that cost money. I tried my best to support my son and daughter with the money in my commissary account. My mother helped out as much as she could, making sure they had what they needed.

A few days before that first Father's Day away from my family, I had an idea. My bunkie, J-Roc, a former member of the Aryan Brotherhood, who was in on a six-number, shot tattoos. It was his prison side hustle. He had a makeshift tattoo gun made of guitar strings. He kept it hidden in the prison wall of our cell. Nobody knew about it. Anyway, we were talking one day, and I told him that I wanted to get some ink.

"What do you want?" he asked.

"I want my children's names on the back of my arms to pay homage to them this Father's Day. If I can't be with them, I want a part of them with me."

J-Roc pulled his tattoo gun from the wall and sterilized the needles (guitar strings) by rubbing two double AA batteries together—causing a spark and then a flame. We found a lookout to keep watch for the prison guards because if we got caught with fresh ink in prison, we would be issued a prison ticket and thrown into the hole. I paid the lookout in food, and if I remember correctly, I also paid J-Roc for his artwork—ten bags of ramen noodles.

When he was done, I had Mikayla tattooed in old English lettering on the back of one arm and Dillon on the back of the other. From that day forward, I have carried my children with me. I love my kids with all my heart, and they both know it. Being away from them was the worst part of my serving my time. I mean, I am a tough guy. I could handle anything that prison life threw at me—the crappy food, the disagreeable inmates—it didn't matter. My children, however, are my Achilles heel. They are all that matter to me.

I think about my own dad a lot these days. Now, I understand why he didn't want me to go into law enforcement. I remember his stories. He told me once how a man shot himself while standing right in front of him. I often wonder how he dealt with the trauma of the job. He must have bottled it up, withheld a lot because of it. My dad didn't drink. I never saw him sit around with a beer in his hand. I don't know how he dealt with it. Maybe he just didn't. And maybe that's why he found it difficult to say the words I always needed to hear.

Fatherhood. It ain't easy!

I may have mentioned that I got divorced in prison. I asked for nothing. I walked away with nothing. And it was okay. It was more than okay. I had my kids, and that was all I needed.

After my release, Dillon asked, "Dad, when you were going through your sentencing, losing everything and knowing that you were going to prison, what kept you from committing suicide?"

Without hesitation, I looked Dillon in the eye and replied, "You and Mikayla. Having you two kids wouldn't allow me to even think of taking my own life. My love for you and your sister is something more special than you will ever know."

Again, I want to leave a legacy for my children, not a liability. I'm so grateful to be their father. They are God's gift and my four-year absence in their life was a real wakeup call that I don't take for

granted. I think about those lost memories each and every day. I think that's why I remained abstinent from drugs and alcohol during those four years. I needed to own that, and I needed to regain the trust of my kids—earn their love back. They were my motivation—they still are. And believe me when I say, there were dark days, man! I had to dig deep to avoid the temptations that were readily available behind those prison walls—alcohol, drugs, sex, cigarettes, and even cell phones. If you had money, those things were accessible.

I didn't see my kids for four years because of my own stupidity. I was too afraid to ask for help. I had too much pride, and honestly, I didn't know how to get the help I needed. Today, my relationship with Mikayla and Dillon is so much stronger … because *they* are so much stronger! It's not lost on me that my kids had to deal with all the negative small-town chatter. We all know how small towns can be. To look at them now, I can see they did not let what others said about me and about our family keep them from becoming their very best. As a father, that makes me so damn proud! I speak to both my kids every day. Not a day goes by that I don't tell them I love them. That love is louder than any of my fears, and I am no longer too tough or proud to ask for help.

SEVEN

GETTING UNCOMFORTABLE

S erving four years in prison added profound lessons in diversity to my life experience. While doing time, I was presented with many different religions and cultures. I have always been intrigued by people, in general, but it wasn't until I was forced to serve time that I really got to know and understand (in a more meaningful way) how others live and pray. It really hit home when I got to know my workout partner, a young, black man in his twenties named Mario. This kid was a gang member, a true "Blood" who had done some serious federal time, involving a drug conspiracy. He was finishing out his sentence at the state penitentiary with me, which is how we got to know each other.

Mario was very intense. He developed a rigorous and structured workout while in federal prison. He was a good fit for me because 1.) He was younger, and 2.) It pushed me to work harder. Some days, we would do a thousand pushups out in the yard. Other days, we would do burpees. I started to pick up his routine. In the beginning, I noticed it would take him a while to get ready to work out. So, one day, I went to his cell and found him kneeling on a rug. He was praying. Mario is Muslim. Intrigued, I asked questions about his religion. I wanted to know more. Because of the attack on America on September 11, 2001, there have been many misconceptions about Muslims. And the more I talked to Mario, the more I realized he was more like me than not. Just like there are good cops, there are bad cops. Just like there are good doctors, there are bad doctors. The same is true of practicing Muslims. There are some good and some bad. Mario taught me that a good Muslim always has a bruise on his forehead from praying so much.

"You must be one of the good ones. You're always praying," I said. "You're so dedicated to Allah. Tell me more."

"Kyle, the best thing you can do is read the Quran," Mario replied, tossing me a crayon to take notes.

One day, I decided to take his advice, and so I dove in and read the Quran from front to back. I explored the differences between the religion I grew up with (Catholicism) and Mario's. I prayed to Jesus Christ. Mario prayed to Allah.

As Ramadan approached, I figured that if I was to truly understand and appreciate Mario's belief system, I should join him in the fast that went from sunup to sundown. Mario was excited! For thirty days, we fasted together, nothing but water throughout the day and one small meal. The trouble with fasting is that all you think about is food. But I wanted to get through it. It was a project for me, and I knew that I would grow as a person because of it. I thought to myself, *if thousands of people can do this every day, why can't I?*

On a side note, some of the worst foods you would ever want to taste come out of the penitentiary kitchen. There were times when the corrections officers would throw their home-cooked food out, and we'd rummage through garbage cans for their scraps and reheat them in the microwave. We were desperate for something good to eat. Yes, there was a time that I ate out of trash cans. I wouldn't lie about such things.

After completing Ramadan and continuing our rigorous workout regime, I dropped a tremendous amount of weight. I got in great shape. I became more disciplined. And the experience itself helped me gain a newfound respect for both Mario and Muslims alike. It made me realize how faithful Muslims are to Allah, their god, their higher power. I also learned a lot about myself, mainly that seeking a better understanding of others made me a better person.

As a Christian, I've never been *that* dedicated to my God … until now. Yeah, I go to church, but I don't even think you need to physically go to church to be a good Christian and have a relationship with Jesus. The church is a symbol of one's faith. I pray every morning, but fasting requires a great deal of mental fortitude and faithfulness—more than I ever considered before. I remember talking to my mom, my ride or die, on the phone about fasting for Ramadan. Concerned, she asked, "You're not becoming Muslim, are you?"

No. I wasn't becoming Muslim. I never got down on the rug and prayed the way Mario prayed. I never even had a rug in my cell. Fasting was good for me. It was a good piece of my prison puzzle.

One thing it helped me realize was that everybody runs to God when they've got a problem. But when things are good and comfortable ... not so much. Prison life made me realize how important it is to be grateful to God in the good times and in bad. And to be vocal about it. Giving glory to God is an important reminder that we can't do this life without Him, though many try. The problem is that people think they are in control and that they can shoulder this life on their own, and that's just not true. The good news is that we don't have to do it in our own strength. God is in control. He can (and will) bear the weight of this world for us, and that's why I have this new mindset. Whether life is hard or freewheeling, I sit in the backseat and let God do the driving. It's just easier that way.

I smile when I hear successful, rich people say that they are "self-made." I laugh and say to myself, "Nah, man! You are God-made!" And there is a difference between being rich and being wealthy. With this newfound knowledge, I consider myself a wealthy man—money or no money. A big part of that is the village I have built up over the years, the people in my life—my children, my family, my new wife, Jennifer, and my personal and professional connections.

Growing up, I never saw a person's color. I saw people as people. However, my career in law enforcement made me cynical and jaded. I stereotyped everybody. After spending time with Mario and completing my thirty-day fast during Ramadan (while reading the Quran), that all went away. I had a higher understanding, and life started to make sense. I started digging into my own religious background. As I mentioned, I was raised Catholic. I attended Catholic school. My dad's side of the family has Jewish roots, but I wouldn't say I practiced my faith.

The real spiritual turning point for me was when I spent thirty days in solitary confinement. It was a dark and dingy place, and the only time I had any type of interaction with anyone was when it was time to eat. I could hear the wheel turning on the concrete floor. During that time, I didn't talk to anybody. I didn't even get to talk to my family on the telephone. Right before Christmas, I tried calling them but got disconnected. I fell to pieces. I wanted to talk to my kids. Nobody knew where I was because I was in Grafton, Ohio, in solitary confinement. It was the worst time in my life, but honestly, it was the greatest time of my prison sentence because it was just God and me in lockup—nobody else. That is when I got close to Him. I decided to drop Catholicism and become a Christian—isolation created elevation within me.

It's where I had to separate where I was going in life from where I wanted to go. I visualized what I would have to do to get there. I knew it would be a long and precarious road. Looking back, those thirty days in solitary confinement prepared me, not only for a relationship with God but for a relationship with myself that included a strong mental state.

Because I was a high-profile prisoner, I started my sentence in protective custody. There were only a few of us, and I couldn't do much. I couldn't even go out in the yard to work out. So, after six months, I signed myself out. I purposefully chose to integrate into the general population. I couldn't deal with being stuck in a small, controlled space for four years. I wasn't living. The warden didn't like my decision, but I took the jump, nonetheless, knowing that I could not return to protective custody if things went badly. I was fine with it and, in the end, it all worked out for the best.

All the prisoners knew who I was as soon as I walked in. They referred to me as "Sheriff." The first day I got out of my cell and walked into the day room, one of the men (a gang member) took me to his cell and offered me drugs. He said, "The first one's on me, next one's on you."

I set the tone as a leader by refusing his offer. I stood my ground, declining drugs, and I got respect for it. Some guys called me Gotti because I was like a boss. It was kind of funny. For the most part, I got along with everybody, including the Bloods and the Aryan Brotherhood. I had no problems with the gang members, except for one, but I handled it the way you do in prison. You go into a cell, and you fight, and take care of it—right then and there. I hate to say it, but you either fight or fuck. It's unfortunate, but you can get raped if you don't stand up for yourself. And it's a constant battle.

When you get your commissary, guys will stand around and wait for your bag. They'll extort you—I was never extorted. I grew up boxing. I was a wrestler. I was in pretty good shape. I was always strong, so I was never afraid to fight when I had to. There were plenty of times when I was a plainclothes detective that I'd end up getting into some gnarly fist fights and altercations. Even then, I handled it like a boss. Never underestimate the quietest guy in the room.

When I met Mario, I really started to move forward with my life. I got involved with some of the prison programs, including Intensive Outpatient Program, Peer Recovery, and addiction studies, and I eventually got my chemical dependency counseling license. I studied addiction as an illness. I even studied business law. I already had a couple of college degrees under my belt, but I suddenly felt compelled to get educated. I immersed myself in knowledge. Every step I took toward bettering myself—in the yard, working out, or in the pages of a book—felt like a necessary shedding, reaching beyond my former self toward a hopeful new existence, as God intended. It felt good, but at the same time, it was incredibly uncomfortable. Even the people I was surrounded by needed a fine-tuned understanding of what it means to be human, to make mistakes, and to love without condition. The irony was not lost on me that I, the former Sheriff of Sandusky County, was holed up with criminals I had made a career out of putting away. Obviously, God's got a sense of humor. Either that or He just knows what a man needs to get his life straight.

I'll never forget my first Thanksgiving in prison. I was invited to make a dish and join a bunch of other inmates for a meal. We all sat around the table and ate together. I looked around at everybody, and I said, "Do you see anything unusual about this?"

"Yeah, you're the only white guy," one guy responded.

"No," I laughed, looking around at the other men and nodding at each one. "Think about it. You're a Blood. You're from the streets of Columbus. You're from Cleveland. Would you guys be eating Thanksgiving dinner together outside of these concrete walls?"

The men shook their heads.

"No," I said. "You'd all be fighting, and chances are, you would be running from me. Why does it take a prison sentence to bring us together?"

"You're right, Kyle," another guy exclaimed.

We broke bread together that day. We learned that we all wanted the same thing—freedom. Many of those men I did time with are still there. They're never getting out. Some have overdosed and died. One guy got out a few months ago and ended up reoffending. I heard he was in a shootout over a burger and was killed. One of the men I got out with did twenty-seven years. He was a good friend of mine. He used to say, "Kyle, I'm innocent."

And I always believed him. Turned out he *was* innocent. So, they let him out. He's married now, with a job, and doing good things. Look, I know we all struggle, and for me to sit here and say that I don't struggle ... I'd be lying. But there is a big difference between experiencing pain and experiencing discomfort. In my life, I can honestly say that I don't know *real* pain. Pain is something big, like when Jesus died on the cross. That is *real* pain.

Discomfort?

Yeah, sure ... I know discomfort. We all do. It's unavoidable. If you're going to change, you've got to get comfortable with the uncomfortable. One of the things I talk to my therapist about is getting uncomfortable. For example, I never wanted to donate blood because I hate seeing needles go into my veins. So, as an exercise, I made myself give blood, and it was good because, in doing so, I saved three lives. Fasting for thirty days in prison was seriously uncomfortable. But it was all about being uncomfortable to achieve something life-altering. You can't put a monetary value on that. Spending four years in prison was extremely uncomfortable, but it was good for me. It changed me ... for the better. It all goes back to God. If you truly have faith in Him, you know that He has your best interest at heart and that He is the *only* judge, so you live your life differently.

The other day, I was talking to an acquaintance of mine, and he asked, "Who do you work for?"

Smiling, I replied, "God's my CEO."

The guy laughed and said, "And we're the board of trustees!"

Amen, brother! Amen!

Friend, all we can do is our best! With the grace of God, everything else is fixable and forgivable. There's no such thing as perfection, only progression. As I work to finish this book, I am back in the gym, hitting it harder than ever. I am following through, doing things differently, and focusing on being more structured. I've turned the heat up a notch. I refuse to get lackadaisical. There is no growth in being lazy and comfortable. Nothing good is going to come of that! You've got to get uncomfortable if you want to grow.

I heard something interesting the other day. Motivational speaker and former athlete, Inky Johnson, said, "You're born looking like your parents, but you die looking like your decisions."

There is a lot of truth in that!

I'm not going to allow myself to become one of those older gentlemen you see sitting at a table, drinking coffee with their retired buddies at McDonald's, looking back at what might have been if only they had stretched their faith a little more.

Most people run from a challenge and adversity. These days, I run to it. I am obsessed with getting uncomfortable. I park further away at the grocery store. I give blood. I do it to get inside my head so that adversity doesn't seem so bad when it hits. Honestly, adversity is one of the greatest gifts God has given me. Why? Because He knows that my challenges are the thing that will bring out my greatest strengths, because it requires that I exercise my faith. It will also draw out my greatest supporters! And the same is true for you!

And if you remember nothing else, remember this: addiction doesn't make you dishonorable. You can be a recovering addict and still have honor and still be a good guy.

I was very outspoken about recovery in prison, doing everything I needed to get through. The other inmates started to gravitate toward me. They were looking for hope. That's when I realized that I could help others.

I am still friends with many of those men I was in prison with, some of whom are or have been released. I believe in second chances. I am a perfect example of what positive change can look like. Even my kids say I am so different from the way I used to be. That's probably the biggest compliment of my life!

EIGHT
CONVICTED-FRIED FELON

On Monday, February 3, 2025, I achieved ten years sobriety. The three things that got me where I am today are God, family, and prison—in that order. It's true—I found peace in prison. You can't put a price on that. While serving my sentence, there was no more chaos in my brain. It was gone. Oh, there was physical chaos all around me with many of the inmates daily. But I found my peace behind those barbed wire fences. I needed it, too.

While on parole, I was expected to get a job. I was lucky to have a friend named Larry Bowman, who owned a couple of Lee's Famous Recipe Chicken restaurants. I reached out to Larry on the off chance he would give me, a convicted felon, a job. During the interview, I was offered a job frying chicken. It only paid $9.50 an hour, but I was ecstatic because 1.) I had to have a job to keep from violating my parole, 2.) It would allow me to pay back over $21,000 in restitution, and 3.) Somebody was willing to take a chance on me.

Number three meant the most!

Fresh out of prison, I was down on myself. I didn't have a place to go. I was homeless, leaning on hopeless. But if, like me, you have spent any time in the Bible, you know that God will provide. Philippians 4:19 reads: "And my God will supply every need of yours according to his riches in glory in Christ Jesus."[3]

Well, the need was answered by a woman named Deb, a librarian who worked at Terra State Community College. Once upon a time, I was on the board of trustees at that college. I'd been appointed by Governor John Kasich of the state of Ohio, if you can believe that! At the time, I got to be good friends with Deb. We always got along well. When I was in prison, she and her girlfriend supported me. They sent me cards and letters, asking if I needed anything. And when I was released, I reached out to her, relying on her kindness.

---

[3] *The Bible*, Philippians 4:19 English Standard Version

"I need a place to stay," I said.

Deb did not hesitate.

"You can come stay with me," she replied.

Deb let me flop on an air mattress in her spare bedroom. I had nothing but six bags of donated clothes from a local halfway house. It turned out to be a good situation. When I was able to get enough money together, I opted to find a cheap apartment in the hood. However, Deb insisted I stay with her. I figured it may have had to do with the fact that her girlfriend had just left her.

"If you want," she said. "You can stay here for free—forever! I don't care. I love your company."

To this day, Deb and I are still very close. I am grateful for her friendship—more than she knows! I was lucky to have found a handful of people who believed in me enough to take me in and offer me work. It was a bit of a risk; I get that. I had gone from the top of the heap (as the youngest sheriff in the state) to the bottom of the heap (a felonious fry cook and recovering addict making minimum wage).

What made me different was that I understood that I was in a state of rebuilding. I knew I had to start somewhere, so with fried chicken batter up to my eyeballs, I swallowed my pride and got humble quick. I had to take responsibility and

move forward. So, I got good at my job. I hustled in the back kitchen, sweating over big vats of hot oil. I got along with a lot of the other employees. There were a couple of us who had served time. Those guys knew me from the streets when I was the sheriff. Things got especially uncomfortable when some of the locals found out I worked as a fry cook. They figured it would be funny to snap photos of me standing over raw chicken parts and grease. They created memes on

Facebook, making jokes out of me and my life choices. They did their best to tear me down, but I'm happy to say they failed miserably. As a matter of fact, all their teasing did was turn me up. I had been through far worse!

While serving my time, I had everything stripped from me. So, for me, frying chicken was a gift. More importantly, it was only temporary. I knew not everybody had it in them to push through that kind of discomfort, but I did. I had God on my side, and I had to show my kids what I could overcome. I couldn't afford to be a failure—not again. It wasn't pain I was feeling—it was discomfort, and that is what spurs greatness, if you have it in you to do something about it. I no longer concerned myself with what others thought of me. I had to believe in myself before anyone else could believe in me. My motto in life these days is this: I never lose—I learn. Let me say that again.

I never lose—I learn.

In life, we are all going to come face-to-face with challenges. It happens every day. Don't look at it as a battle or a failure. Look at it as a lesson. I learned that I needed to be stripped of everything to find out who I was at my core. That was part of God's plan, and if frying chicken was a part of that plan, then so be it! By remaining patient and obedient to His purpose for my life, each day only got better. I found I was no longer having bad days, just bad moments. I had learned to shake that shit off, and that changed everything!

Yes, I'm a convicted felon. Maybe I wasn't supposed to come out of this situation better than I was before. But because I believe anything is possible, especially with God, I was able to keep going! I've had some real setbacks in my life, but I learned from them. I learned two very important things: 1.) I've got to be more patient, and 2.) I've got to be more obedient. If I can achieve those two things, I'm certain good things will follow.

Patience and obedience are two very difficult things to achieve in the world we live in, where instant gratification is king. If I could sit for four years in prison and find peace, I sure as heck could fry chicken for as long as it took for me to move ahead. Believe me when I say, there's more to come. And I'm not talking about obtaining material wealth—I'm not driven by riches. I want wealth, as it relates to memories with friends and family, and the things in life that truly matter, like giving back.

In prison, we were given state pay that equaled $27 a month. It sounds trivial, but we looked forward to it. It meant we could go to the commissary and stock up on food and goods. Some of us could go weekly and change up our food supply. Some weren't as privileged— or should I say "blessed" to have additional financial support from outside the prison walls. I was very aware of how blessed I was in prison, and I wanted to give back when I could. There were a lot of people who were struggling in lockup, men who didn't have family, commissary money, or provisions. I once traded two boxes of laundry detergent for a television set. I turned around and gave that television to somebody who didn't have anything. And just before I was released, I gave all my stuff away, except for my prison blanket and my Timberland boots. I walked a lot of miles in those boots around the prison yard. I bought them from another inmate in exchange for commissary items. I kept them as a reminder of my journey. I still wear them to this day, though on a far different path. And if I ever step foot in a prison yard again, it will be in those boots to share my story with inmates.

I no longer take anything for granted because, in the blink of

an eye, if I were to screw up again, I could be right back behind those

walls, in a six-by-nine cell—stripped of all the things that matter most.

NINE
TWO FENCES TO FREEDOM

rison was not punishment; it was God's preparation for my life's purpose. I know that now. Oh, and by the way, I didn't find God, He found me when I was at my lowest point. When I was sent to the penitentiary, I was mad at God. I was angry, always asking Him, "Why me?"

Today, I know the answer. I had to crawl through the mud to understand my purpose. This journey wasn't by chance. God chose me. I believe that with my whole heart, and I take full responsibility for my addiction and all the things that I did to land me in prison, including my infidelities to my first wife and stealing prescriptions from my parents. God had to break me down to get me where he needed me to be. He doesn't just crown His children without first having asked them to demonstrate faith in the waiting season—timing is everything! And in the process, He breaks them down, and only through their faith in Him does He crown them with favor and abundance. I needed to be broken down. Those first thirty days in solitary confinement were my rock bottom. It's where I got to know God—really know Him. Even though I was still questioning everything, God was there with me. He put His hands on me, and he said, "Listen to me, Kyle. You need to be here. This is all a part of My plan."

I heard Him say those words.

In the hole, all I had was time and space to listen to God and hear what He had to say. That's the *only* reason I was able to navigate prison life. God was in lockup with me. He never left my side. He led me through the wilderness. Time is one of the most valuable assets in the world. You can't buy it. It's priceless. But if you're patient, and you take the time to listen in the quiet, really listen, God will lead you through the hard times, too. I believe that now more than I did in 2016, when I was first incarcerated, and my world collapsed all around me. I often wonder how I got through the indictment and those hearings.

I wonder how I got through those first few days in prison.

God was there with me—that's how.

That's the truth. I couldn't have done it on my own. I was broken. I had people in my community backing me, and that was good. But having Him behind me made me limitless. I heard God's voice inside those prison walls. I had conversations with Him, especially during those first thirty days when I was in solitary confinement. I never prayed so hard in all my life!

As I mentioned before, I was raised Catholic. I basically went through the motions in my spiritual life, but today my faith has been forged in my salvation. Prayer has become my routine, and it changed me. I can remember lying in my bunk every night, praying for my family, praying for my children, praying for my salvation. I never did that before. I was forty-two years old when I was incarcerated, and all those years before, I never prayed! Not for any reason. That's why I don't think of my prison sentence as punishment. It was preparation. God was getting my attention. He reached out to me, and I finally listened. If I hadn't, I wouldn't be here today. I truly believe that! That initial thirty-day isolation created elevation. My time in solitary confinement got me closer to God and the truth. He planted a seed in me. I used to envision myself speaking and being interviewed on podcasts. I didn't even know what a podcast was back then. I pictured myself sharing my story, helping people on their own journey from addiction to purpose. Sure, when I got out, I had rough spells, but those rough spells were part of the test and preparation to move me forward. I was preparing for my purpose.

Faith over fear is a powerful thing. It's all about trusting God in the good times and the bad. I believe addiction is the devil, and the closer we get to God and our God-given purpose, the harder the devil fights to conquer our flesh. The devil still whispers in my ear from time to time, but I pay him no mind. I've got my eyes so strongly on God right now, and the devil knows it. Believe me when I say, he'll chase you down when you work to please God. He knows you are a meant for more, strong and powerful, and he wants to keep you from God's glory. It's that simple.

There were plenty of times I could have caved and started using drugs again. It's not hard to get high in prison, but I stayed focused on the fact that my prison time was preparation for something bigger. It wasn't easy, especially during the holidays. I knew my family was gathering, and I couldn't be there.

I refused to feel sorry for myself or allow my weak moments to lead me to temptation. Freedom from addiction was the biggest weight lifted off my shoulders. Even behind bars, I could walk freely and look myself in the proverbial mirror every day. I was proud of who I was becoming. If nothing else, I had owned the addiction. I named it before it claimed me and made me another sad statistic. The shame was no longer hanging over my head. I was at peace without the pills. I could walk around the yard with my head held high. It didn't matter that I still had time to serve or that I had gone from sheriff to felon. And it didn't matter what anyone else said or thought about me. I was going to be okay.

Along the perimeter of the prison were two fences, making it twice as hard to escape. The other inmates and I walked along those two fences every day. I always focused beyond the chain links and contemplated my freedom and what it meant to me. I would wonder what my family and friends were doing without me. I watched the sunset from behind those two fences, trying to visualize the people I loved most in the world, watching that same sunset. I knew someday I would get out, and so I imagined what I would be doing outside of those two fences. It was in those small moments that I found hope. Of course, there were days when I didn't want to leave my cell. In the beginning, I just laid around in my bunk and felt sorry for myself. It was awful. Then one day, a fellow inmate pulled me aside and said, "I see what you're doing, Kyle. Don't do it, man!"

"What?" I asked.

"Man, when I first got locked up, I was sent to the doctor to get some bloodwork done. When it came back, I was told that I was HIV positive. I had lived a clean life, but because of a physical altercation with someone who was HIV positive, I got infected."

This man, whom I had gone to Bible study with behind bars, told me that even though his sentence was shorter than mine, his days were literally numbered.

"Be thankful you don't have my battle," he said. "Do your time and then go live your life. You're going to be okay."

That conversation changed how I looked at my life. I needed it, too. God used that man to deliver an important message and that was to keep my eyes on Him—the Man Upstairs. That sounds easy, but boy, did I have some rough days. I didn't feel I had much purpose. But God never gave up on me, not even after I lied, cheated, stole, and got angry with Him. If I learned anything, I learned that God is always going to test you, but fear not! The test is what sharpens and develops your greatest strengths. I believe that. I no longer ask God, "Why me?" Instead, I ask, "Why not me?"

TEN
LOVE, MOM

My mom has always been and will always be my ride or die. From the beginning, she has shown up for me. There were always holes in me and my dad's relationship. Where my mom was affectionate, my dad was old school in his parenting style. In other words, he was indifferent. I had to accept that. He would often tell my mom, "Kyle's your project."

In his defense, I was a little different as a child. Even though I was into sports, I was always a bit offbeat. I was artistic and thought outside the box. I'm not sure my dad knew what to do with that. My mom, however, always supported me. She has never given up on me! When I was applying to the art program at the University of Toledo, Mom went with me to deliver my portfolio at the Toledo Museum of

Art campus. When I needed somebody to ride with me to powerlifting competitions, she was the one. She was there when I won the Ohio State Championship at nineteen years old. She was there when I switched over to bodybuilding. She prepped my meals and grilled chicken breast like it was going out of style.

Mom was the "runner," the one who ran us kids to school, sporting events, church, you name it. At church, I served as an altar boy. On weekday mornings, she got me up bright and early for seven o'clock mass. Mom sat in the pews, praying and making sure I was on time to serve our Lord and Savior. While Dad was out providing for the family, Mom was planted in the bleachers, pews, and deep in our corner. The woman made me breakfast every morning before I went to school—eggs and toast. We grew up out in the country. We had chickens, which meant we had fresh eggs. Most kids I knew didn't get that. As for me, it was eggs (sunny side up) and buttered toast— always! Whatever I was into, Mom supported me one hundred and ten percent! She sacrificed her time and energy, regardless of the fact that she also worked as a librarian at St. Anne's Elementary School and at Mosier Construction to earn extra money for the family.

Years later, after my bond was revoked, I surrendered to the authorities. At that point, my mom knew everything there was to know about my addiction, my marriage, my infidelities, and so forth. I was still in denial—the shame was just too much to bear. But as far as my mom was concerned, there was no shame. I knew that no matter what I had done, she loved and accepted me without fail. That was one of the best feelings in the world!

When I was sent to prison, Mom never turned her back on me. When I'd call home from the penitentiary, she would always pick up the phone. And she always answered the tough questions, and when she couldn't, she would simply say, "Everything's going to be alright."

And I always believed her because if she was saying it, it had to be true. I trusted my mom with everything. She accepted my addiction and all my flaws. She was there throughout my four-year prison sentence. She showed up with my father for visits, to see if I needed anything. She cared for my children when I was inside. She sent me greeting cards in the mail, and they were always signed, "Love, Mom."

When I got out of prison, I had her signature "Love, Mom" tattooed on my arm. That way, when she is gone, I will always have her with me. I can't even think about it without tears welling up in my eyes. My mom is strong, wise, beautiful, intelligent, and a hard worker. She's the best! It's going to hurt when I lose her. I just hope she is as close to God as I am.

Because of her, I know what love is and what being a parent means, and I am the same way with my children. I never miss an opportunity to tell Mikayla and Dillon that I love them. When my mom and I discussed my addiction, she blamed herself, saying that she should have known.

If you're reading this, Mom ... it's not your fault.

It's mine, and I take full responsibility.

I apologized for everything, and she forgave me everything and more. When I was in prison, my mom bought a book on addiction to better understand the disease. She wanted to understand me and where I was going in my life. That simple act speaks volumes about her. My mom's willingness to dive deep into her son's addiction (without judgement) was a whole other level of love. She could have turned her back on me and said, "Kyle is a drug addict. There is nothing I can do."

But she didn't.

To this day, she tells me that she is proud of me.

I am so grateful for that.

My mom had a lot of experience with addiction. It ran on her side of the family. My uncle, who is also my godfather, did twenty-seven years in prison for his dealings with drugs. My mom stuck close to him, too. She never stopped loving him. She's a fighter in that way!

Maybe that's where I get my fighting spirit.

Fortunately, for my uncle, he's out now and works in recovery. He has done wonders in his career, and I'm very proud of him. He's an amazing man! I'm sure much of that has to do with my mother's love and devotion. I know I am changed by it.

My mom gave me life, and growing up, she never stopped speaking life into me. Without her, I would not be who I am today. I am blessed. Women like her don't come around often, which is why we should never, ever take our parents for granted. If your parents are still around today, grab a hold of them and don't let them go. Treat them with all the love and respect because they deserve it.

My mom is a gift from God. I love her with all my heart, and I always will. Her infinite love, unwavering support, and unshakeable faith in me have been a perpetual source of motivation. Her wisdom has been nothing short of life-transforming! It's no wonder her name is Cheryl, which in French means "beloved." To this day, whenever we speak, Mom's last words to me are always, "I love you, Kyle!"

You may say that I'm an emotional man, especially when it comes to life and love, and you'd be right. This is the most passionate I've ever been. That's how I know what I am writing about is real. If I wasn't emotional about this stuff, if I didn't cry talking about it, then I'd be living a lie.

ELEVEN
SMOKEY'S LOVE

mokey and I have had a rollercoaster of a relationship. From childhood, I was always my "mom's project." I was an art guy. My dad didn't quite get me, so I did my own thing. I worked out. I got into bodybuilding and powerlifting. I went to art school and then I did something nobody saw coming. I went into law enforcement like my dad, and I went straight to the top. Even though he didn't want that life for me, he was proud of me.

I'll never forget that first visit with Smokey in prison. He and my mom came down to see me. During that visit, I looked at my dad, and I asked, "What do you think, Dad?"

Smokey looked me in the eye and replied, "You know what to do—you make it right."

I knew what he meant. My dad was wise and often spoke in metaphors. He'd say things like, "I'm too old a cat to get screwed by a kitten," "If it's free, it's for me," and "Don't work for the system; let the system work for you."

One thing that he always said that I kept in my back pocket was, "Treat others the way you want to be treated, and you'll go far." I never forgot that one, especially when I was incarcerated with the same people I had put into prison. Having been on both sides of the prison fence, Dad was right. I was better able to relate to others because of that simple piece of advice—"treat others the way you want to be treated." That's the Golden Rule according to the Bible.

Upon my release from prison, my dad never shunned or shamed me. Nor did he ever tell me that he loved me. I've always struggled with that. I mean, deep down, I know my dad loves me. But to never have heard the words "I love you, son," said out loud is something that I can't get past. My therapist says that it could be a generational thing—not that it helps me absolve the hurt I feel. I know my dad is proud of me for the work I am doing today. I talk to him about it all the time. But letting him down the way I did, when I was sent to the penitentiary, was one of the hardest things I've ever had to overcome. I have been chasing Smokey's love and approval my whole life—**my whole life!** As much as it hurts not to hear the words, I am a better father because of it. Since the day my kids were born, even when I was locked up, I told my kids that I love them. I tell them all the time now. I even tell my dad that I love him, to which he replies, "Okay."

I am so grateful for my father. If it wasn't for him, I wouldn't be the man I am today—a closet artist, turned former law enforcement officer, turned addiction recovery advocate. I suppose that says a lot about my relationship

with my dad, my need for his approval, and the man I am still aiming to become. Even to this day, I am working hard to get back on top of my game. I know I am capable of it, and I think deep down, my dad

knows I am, too. And that's enough for me.

TWELVE
STIGMA AF

Recovery is different for everybody. Some folks need five meetings a week, others two. Some are admitted into treatment centers, while others quit addiction just as easily as someone else might quit going to the gym. As for me, I never received addiction treatment, perse. My recovery began behind bars, while I was incarcerated and living in a six-by-nine cell. I survived on ramen noodles from the commissary, three-square meals a day, and hope for a better life.

My first month in prison was spent in solitary confinement. It was just me, myself, and I—no Oxycontin, Percocet, Vicodin, or girlfriend to dull the pain. It was a jumpstart into recovery, and as rough as it was, it was necessary to get my head right. The hardest part was being left alone with my thoughts and feelings of regret. No one but God to talk to. No one to blame but myself. No way out of the mess I had created. I had to go through it.

These days, I talk to a therapist. It helps, but the thing that really keeps me juiced up (driving my healing), is my life's work. I am in the industry of recovery. Helping people is my medicine now, my drug of choice. Every time I am able to facilitate healing for someone else, that release of dopamine keeps me going. When I am able to walk hand in hand with others in their recovery, people who are going through what I went through and worse, my purpose is reinforced and intensified—it keeps me sober. I wake up clean every morning, and I am grateful!

I stick close to Narcotics Anonymous. I read my Bible. I offer others an ear or a word of encouragement, a piece of myself and my story, and it doesn't matter if it's in a Narcotics Anonymous meeting, a team meeting, or in line at the grocery store—I stop, and I listen to people. I give them the time of day. I give of myself in that way. That has been the greater part of my recovery journey. It doesn't hurt that

I have a beautiful wife to go home to, a woman who supports me unconditionally. I am finally free!

And I'm not even talking about being kicked out of "government housing." I'm talking about owning my life story, never again falling prey to those pretty, little pills and the promises they make. I am redeemed—God delivered me through all of it and not because I deserved it, because I didn't— I don't. God saved me so that I could fulfill His purpose for my life, to lead others to Him in their recovery.

It's winter in Ohio as I write this, and I still struggle with the pain of arthritis. The pain is worse in the cold, and it reminds me of where I used to be—rock bottom—seeking the next fix, the next refill on the third of every month. The pain reminds me of how I manipulated and lied to feed that awful pang of addiction growing inside of me. The ache for it takes me back to that six-by-nine cell, where it all came to a head and where God came into my life.

Addiction took me away from my family—I will never let that happen again. It's easier for me to say that now than it was in the beginning. I'd see commercials on television, advertising pills for this and that. I'd overhear prisoners talking about Percocet, and I would reminisce fondly as though they were talking about a woman I once wooed. I'd hear a song on the radio, and I was reminded of all the times I'd hunch over the newly refilled pill bottle—the tremor in my hands, my thick fingers fumbling with the childproof cap, the rattle of the bottle, and the faint whiff of desperation when I'd dig through the cotton to get to the pills. It was an unrequited romance of sorts—me longing for relief that never came from a drug that never returned my desire. Like so many love stories, it didn't end well—but it could have ended much worse, I suppose.

I was so ashamed. I saw myself as someone who wore two scarlet letters—**"A" for addict** and **"F" for felon**. I was no longer Kyle Overmeyer—Sandusky County Sheriff. I was 692183. I was a number. Overcoming that stigma was one of the biggest challenges of my life. What I came to realize was that addicts aren't necessarily bad people. Oftentimes, their addiction and mental health (if not treated) can lead to criminal behavior, arrests, misdemeanors, felonies, prison time, and even death. Not everyone understands that. I suppose there was a time as sheriff that I didn't understand that either, which is why I have made it my mission to help people (i.e., legislators) understand addiction as a disease. I think it's important to shatter the stigma.

There are times I still struggle with the idea that I wore an ankle monitor, fried chicken for a living, and flopped on someone's air mattress while I got back on my feet. Mostly, I struggle to forgive myself. It's my twenty-two-year-old son, Dillon, who stops me and says, "Dad, why are we even talking about it? It's over."

It's interesting to me that someone so young can understand forgiveness so well. As his father, I'd love to take the credit, but my son is definitely coming into his own. Much like my daughter, Mikayla, who now has a family of her own. I am so proud of my kids. Life has a way of shaping us all, sanding down the rough edges, ironing out the wrinkles, and making us the men and women we were meant to become.

I am here to encourage you, if not assure you, that you can reinvent yourself. You are not defined by your past mistakes. You can choose to be the greatest or the worst version of who you are right now. I chose to be the greatest. And that's what I strive and hustle for every day! I want to break the stigma. I want to be a better man. I want to leave a legacy for my family, not a liability. It's taken a lot of work to get here. And there is so much more to do.

In 2017, while serving my sentence, I wrote a goodbye letter to my addiction. It was a part of my healing process. It reads:

Dear Ms. Opiate,

It has been a very long time since we last crossed paths. Over three years ago, I permanently told you goodbye. The end of our relationship was my new beginning to a clean and sober life.

I still remember the first time you were introduced to me. Due to my chronic arthritis, the doctor prescribed you. As advised, I needed you every day to make my physical pain go away. There wasn't a day that you were not by my side. I began my mornings with you, and we ended our nights together as well. Unfortunately, I began to need you more and more. When I couldn't find you at one doctor, I would look for you at another. If I couldn't find you in Vicodin, then you were sure to be in Percocet.

When we were together, it was a happy place. You knew just how to take all the blues away. Eventually, it felt like you loved me, but you deceived me. It was just a façade, but it was too late. My use had already evolved into addiction. On top of everything else, my compulsion and need for you led me to my current destination, incarceration. If you think I'm sad or struggling, you are totally incorrect. The demise that you presented to me became my uprise. Since being in prison, I am no longer in denial and have accepted my addiction.

My family and friends have forgiven me, but most importantly, I have forgiven myself. I am perfectly aligned with this adverse event in my life, as it is both a lesson and a blessing. I have instilled power, peace, happiness, and direction. I have found my true purpose in life.

In closing, this letter was not written because I miss or need you, not by any means. This letter was written to remind you to lose my phone number, address, email address, and every other form of communication. You are absolutely not welcome in my life again. I never want to see you again. Get lost, Ms. Opiate!

Sincerely,

Kyle Overmyer, #692183

THIRTEEN
THE MISSING PIECE OF THE PUZZLE

My official release date from prison on was April 6, 2020. I experienced hardships soon after. I became homeless and was sleeping on an air mattress in a woman's spare bedroom. I had no residence, an ankle monitor, and I was on parole. I started counseling and was working midnight shifts, frying chicken for minimum wage. I was sharing my journey and my outlook on recovery on social media, and one random Sunday in November, a woman named Jennifer reached out to me. We were connected through a high school friend of mine.

I'll never forget that day. I was working out in the gym when I received a message that read: "Hey, I really love your story. I've been following you. I get up north sometimes, and I have worked in the nonprofit field a little bit. I really love helping people. I love redemption stories, and I would love to meet with you and your girlfriend—grab lunch and talk."

Of course, I messaged back with "LOL," explaining to Jennifer that I did not have a girlfriend, but I would be happy to meet for lunch. I still have a screenshot of that message on my phone because this incredible woman became a big piece of my journey.

Jennifer and I chatted back and forth for a while, and then one evening, we spoke on the phone from nine o'clock at night until four in the morning. Our connection was immediate. She was so transparent about who she was and what she had overcome. As for me, in case you haven't noticed, I wear my heart on my sleeve.

What really intrigued me about Jennifer was that she didn't hold back. She wasn't scared of my prison record or my past. In fact, she embraced it. She didn't judge me, and that's how I knew—she was the one.

The day before Thanksgiving, Jennifer drove up to Fremont and spent the night. At that point, I had an apartment in the hood, the same neighborhood where I used to kick in doors as the Sheriff. She was so full of grace. Her son was with his father for the holiday, so that visit turned into a seven-day stayover. We got some Bob Evans takeout, went back to my apartment, and spent our first Thanksgiving together. We went to see a Christmas tree lighting ceremony in Fremont. Everything had come full circle. Jenn and I fell in love, and I remember her asking, "Kyle, what are you doing on January 2, 2021?"

"I don't know," I replied.

"It's a Saturday. Do you want to get married?"

I couldn't believe my ears.

I smiled and said, "Yeah, let's get married!"

There was no hesitation on my part. I knew she was it for me. I mean, I was fresh out of prison, on parole, homeless, and had lost everything! Seriously, if I wanted to leave the state, I had to check in with the police department. I told her everything and shared what I wanted to do with my life, and she never flinched. She believed in me and my vision. She supported me, and we were determined to make it work no matter what. God knows it takes a special kind of woman to love me—so He sent her.

I believe that!

Jennifer ordered a wedding dress on Amazon. She found a photographer and a preacher, a guy from Pickerington, Ohio, where she graduated from high school. Jenn's sister, Andrea, helped us with all the details. I didn't tell anybody on my side of the family, not even my parents and children. It was a lot to spring on them all at once, having just been released from prison.

I was rebuilding my life from the foundation of recovery, so it was interesting (and quite special to me) that Jenn and I were married on Serenity Farms in Lancaster, Ohio. I love the Serenity Prayer so much. I got a tattoo of it on my left bicep.

We had a small reception at Buckeye Lake Winery in Thornville, Ohio with Jenn's mom and her kids in attendance. It couldn't have been a more perfect day.

I was making $11.50 an hour at the behavioral treatment center. I was going to have to commute up north an hour and a half to see her on the weekends in Sunbury, just outside of Columbus. I really believe God was working in my life because seven days later, after we were married, we were eating pizza in Fremont, and the phone rang. It was a job offer in Columbus, working in the field of business development for addiction and mental health. Score!

God's plans are always greater than our own plans. It sounds cliché, but it's true. Look, I know that I am a lot to take. I am so full of energy and positivity ninety-nine percent of the time. I'm the guy who always sees the cup half full. And I think sometimes those kinds of people are harder to deal with than the negative kind. Some folks might think my energy is too much or that it is fake.

There ain't nothing fake about it.

It's not that I don't have down moments. I do, but I don't have down days anymore. There are no bad days for me, just bad moments. I am grateful that Jenn knows how to love me. She accepts me for who I am and all the energy that comes with it. She doesn't pull any punches with me though. She has rolled her eyes at me when I get emotional, poetic, or say too much about what I am feeling.

That's how I show my love.

Jennifer is my best friend. I've never had such an openly communicative relationship like this one. Who would have ever known that five and a half years ago—fresh out of prison, homeless and frying chicken—my life would be this rich and beautiful? I couldn't do it without this woman. I wouldn't want to. There's just no way.

Every morning, I show my wife gratitude. I get up and go get her a large Diet Coke from McDonald's. I don't care if it's 5:00 a.m.; I make sure she's always got it in hand. And I always send her a message every day, letting her know that I love her and that I hope that she has a great day! I tell her that she's the best because she is!

I call her JoJo—that's my pet name for her. I have it tattooed on my left bicep, in her penmanship, inside a puzzle piece, near the Serenity Prayer and my mom's signature. JoJo is the last missing piece of my puzzle. She went back to school to get her college degree. I was so proud of her because she always wanted to finish her education. And she did so, within a year—on her own. Now, she teaches third graders at a Christian academy. Jenn puts her whole heart and soul into those eight-year-olds, and they love her for it!

One of the things I love most about her is that she is a believer in Jesus Christ, too. A couple of years ago, we got baptized together. That is something I will never forget. True companionship (i.e., marriage) works best when you have a partner who also has a strong belief in God and is prepared to take that walk of faith beside you. As a couple, it makes you stronger. This is Jenn's third marriage and my second. She always tells me that the third time is the charm. I always reply, "Not for me! There ain't gonna be a third time."

She's a keeper!

This woman is so loving, generous (sometimes too generous), unselfish, humble, and has an amazing singing voice! She always knows how to make me feel better when I am having a bad moment. She also knows how to give constructive criticism, too. After a speaking gig, whether it's Ohio State Law School, a national healthcare executive dinner, a panel of physicians, or a prison, I will go up to Jenn and ask, "How'd I do? On a scale of one to ten?"

Sometimes she'll simply shrug, as if I could have done better. Or she will knit her brow as she reflects and reply, "Hmmm … I'd give you a seven or eight."

She's real with me, and I love that. The one thing she always does is tells me that she is proud of me. It's great to hear those words, but if I am being honest, it's in the way that she looks at me and smiles,  the way she hugs me and holds my hand, the way she kisses me and accepts me for the flawed man that I am. She just loves me. She is the most beautiful part of God's plan for my life. After her, there are no more bones left in my closet. Jenn got the best version of me—drug-free, tried and true. She must have known that I am a man in progress; she never would have married me otherwise. She inspires me every day to work on myself, to go to therapy, to journal, to give back, and to thank God for every blessing. It's been six years since I was released from prison, and there is much to be thankful for!

FOURTEEN
KO ADDICTION

I was getting a lot of attention on social media. There were a lot of people reaching out to me, who could relate to my story. They were asking for help. The president of the Local Exchange Club, a community-based organization whose focus is on service, fellowship, and idea exchange, reached out to me. He was a family

friend. He invited me to lunch one day and said, "Hey, Kyle! I love what you're talking about! Would you ever consider speaking at the Exchange?"

I was fresh out of prison. I didn't have much, so I had nothing to lose. He barely got the invite out when I exhaled, "Yeah?!"

Mind you, there was some hesitation on my part, because I was once a member of the Exchange. These were people I had betrayed, stolen pills from, manipulated, and lied to at the height of my addiction. The president sensed my reluctance and said, "I think you need to do this."

So, I did, and it was like magic! People asked me questions. They embraced me. They showed me grace because I had shared my story. They understood. Back then, my speaking was much rawer and off the cuff. I have evolved a lot since that day at the Exchange. But I can tell you that speaking in front of those folks was healing.

I let it all out.

Shame is like a scab—it eventually heals and falls off on its own. From then on, more people started reaching out, inviting me to share my story.

My second speaking gig was in Tiffin, Ohio, for a recovery organization. Two of my biggest supporters, my mom and my friend, Ohio State Representative Haraz Ganbari, joined me. They both wanted to hear me speak. Again, my mom has always been my ride or die, and Haraz … he never left my side while I was in prison. He often wrote me letters, encouraging me.

As speaking opportunities increased, it was Jenn who came up with "KO Addiction" as a name for my speaking business. I came home one day, and she said, "You know, now that people are asking you to speak, you need a name for this business. How about KO Addiction?"

It was a brilliant idea—fitting! As a kid, I boxed, and everybody called me KO—short for Kyle Overmyer and Knock Out! I loved it, and I loved her for supporting me so unconditionally.

I'm a lucky man—I married brains and beauty!

I was excited about the idea of sharing my story to those who needed to hear it. I was no stranger to public speaking. Being the sheriff, I knew how to speak in front of crowds. I spoke at a lot of events, rallies, and debates. One year, I delivered the commencement speech for Terra State Community College. I have never shied away from being in front of a crowd. In fact, the more people I have in front of me, the better. I love speaking. I love sharing and engaging with the crowd.

It's kind of my thing.

Two years ago, right before Christmas, I was giving a keynote address in a Washington courthouse. As I was being introduced, ready to run up to the stage, this woman stood up and called out my name. A little boy was sitting next to her.

"Whoa, whoa," she exclaimed. "You can't go up until I speak with you. Do you see this boy?"

I looked over at Jenn in the audience. I was thinking to myself, *that ain't my kid.*

"I came for a reason," she said. "Do you remember your bunkie, J-Roc? He is backing down his eighth number."

"Yeah," I said, beads of sweat forming on my brow.

"Do you remember helping his baby mama?"

"Yes," I replied.

"After overdosing on fentanyl. This little boy found her and called 911. She reached out to you because of J-Roc. You helped get her into treatment and get her clean. I came here tonight to thank you for saving his mom."

I started to cry. The woman approached the stage and hugged me. That was the best Christmas gift I ever got! God knew what he was doing when He started working in my life. Hearing from that woman was when I knew I was on the right path. It literally hit me like a ton of  bricks! I've spoken over fifty times since then. I've been paid up to

$5,000 to give one keynote address, but those aren't even the best ones. It's the times I speak for free that are my favorite. I never turn down an opportunity to speak—paid or not.

I recently proposed to the director of the Ohio Department of Rehabilitation and Correction, who works for the governor, that I go on a tour of all twenty-eight prisons in the state of Ohio. Her eyes lit up, and she asked, "Are you serious?"

"Yes, and I'm not going to charge you," I replied. "I just want to give back."

"Come with me right now," she said. "I want you to meet somebody."

And that's how my Ohio prison speaking tour got started. I've been to eight already, only twenty more to go—and one county jail. I do two a month, knowing that I can make a big impact on these guys. My main message to them is that their past does not define them—it refines them. And if I can come out of this a better man, they can, too!

A man's got to have hope!

I was the disgraced sheriff, the last kid picked to be on a sports team (i.e., dodgeball, baseball, football). Based on my history, I shouldn't have been picked for this opportunity to share my story. But it was God's plan; it wasn't mine. Folks will come up to me and say, "Congratulations, man! You're self-made!"

Nah, man!

I'm God-made. God created me in His image. It's got nothing to do with me. I'm just being obedient. If I could go back to the days when I was Sheriff, when I thought I had everything under control (in my own strength), I would say, "There is something bigger happening here. You are not doing this in your own strength, and don't ever be too proud to ask for help."

Listen, if you are struggling to hear God, you've got to drop down on your knees and pray—hard. That's the only answer—prayer. Alone, you can't control shit. You really can't. I don't care what anybody says or how tough you think you are in this moment. Now, I talk to God every day.

Every. Single. Day.

It took going to prison for me to figure out that I had zero control in life and in lockup. There were times when I made an outgoing call to someone, and the person on the other end of the line would get fed up with me and hang up. Not only was I out eighty-three cents, but I was out a friend. I couldn't text back or drive to their house. I was done—S.O.L.

That's prison life, friend!

So, when I say I had zero control, I mean there was nothing I could do to fix what needed to be fixed outside of myself.

God, on the other hand, has never hung up on me. I can always call (and count) on Him. That's why He is my CEO and Savior. I work for Him. I got nobody else. Now, I know what you're thinking. I've got Jenn, and I've got to answer to her.

Don't get it twisted now. Ha!

Communication in marriage is the key to success—that and grit. But God … He's my main Man! In the midst of my addiction, trauma, and mental health issues, I held a lot of things inside. I have since learned to let go of the shame and the pride.

I let go, and I let God.

Why? Because I believe God had a plan for my life long before I was even conceived. And He never, ever gave up on me between that day and now. I'm a fifteen-time felon who was just voted in to sit on a prestigious board that was started by Governor Bob Taft's wife, Hope Rothert Taft. There is no way I could have managed this on my own—not if I tried. This is God at work.

Let me tell you something: God doesn't give his children more than they can't handle. He might not always answer our prayers in a way that we think He should, or in the timing that we hope for, but He is always there, and He is never late! There will be seasons in your life that you don't understand why you're going through some hard times, but there will come a day, not long down the road, that you will realize why you had to go through it.

When I was in the thick of my addiction, I didn't understand why I was suffering so badly, but I do now. Adversity is a gift. The life I have now is so much more than I could have ever imagined. I married the woman of my dreams. I have a relationship with my children. I speak on a topic near and dear to my heart to people who are interested in what I have to say. I love my life!

So, keep your head up and stay the course. Have faith in God—He has already handled the struggle you are currently facing. You just have to believe and give Him praise every single day—in the good and in the bad. I'm a different man than I used to be. I am a stronger man. It's because I no longer fear—I am too full of faith.

I will admit, however, that I cry a whole lot more than I used to when I was younger. But I believe God gave us tears for joy, just as he did for sadness and pain. Now and then, I'll get a jolt in church when I read a passage, or listen to a sermon, or see humanity in action.

The other night, while Jenn and I were driving in the car, we were listening to the radio. A young man was sharing a story about how he had experienced the warmth and generosity of an elderly couple at a restaurant. He told how he had noticed a woman struggling with her meal because of dementia, and how her husband took care of everything for her.

Moved by what he had seen, the man decided to treat the couple to dessert, so he asked his waitress to send one over. He admired how this man took care of his wife. When he got up to pay the bill for his own meal (and the couple's dessert), the waiter told him that his meal had been taken care of by the couple who had been treated to a slice of cake. Hearing this, I immediately started crying.

That's God stuff right there!

When I was Sheriff, I never shed a tear, not even when we pulled those boys out of the river, not when I was involved in an officer-involved shooting, and not when I was arrested on forty-three counts. On the outside, I was Teflon tough—non-stick emotions. The truth is, I was more like Tupperware, holding every emotion I felt hostage in an airtight container. It was suffocating—destructive. Nowadays, I'll hear a song on the radio, or I'll look into my wife's eyes, and I'll start crying. Jenn just looks at me, shakes her head, and asks, "What's wrong with you?"

Lady, how much time do you have?

FIFTEEN
LEAVES OF CHANGE

After spending four years in prison, I no longer wear a watch, and I don't think I ever will again. There is no room for it in my life. No disrespect to some of the great timepieces out there, but there's just no use for it—not for me. Now, I look at time as the most priceless currency, and no watch in the world will keep me from simply appreciating the time I have left.

While doing time, we prisoners were ruled by the clock. We would sit in the bay room, watching the minutes and hours slowly tick by. After a while, that got old. Some guys would keep a calendar, marking down the days left of their sentence. I never did. I knew how much time I had. I didn't need a reminder, so I quickly decided to stop watching the clock. It would only make my sentence feel longer. A lot of my time was spent working out. Afterward, I'd walk the track in the prison yard with some of the guys. There was a wooded area just outside the prison walls, and one day I looked up and saw that the leaves were starting to change. It was so beautiful, and that's when I realized that I never really stopped to notice that change of season before. I never looked at those things. From that moment on, the leaves became my clock, because each time the colors changed, it meant that I was one more year down in my sentence. And guess what? One year turned into two years, and then, of course, three years, and finally ... four.

I was sentenced to prison when I was forty-two years old, and in all my years, I never looked at nature in that way. It was a sad realization that I never appreciated some of the beautiful things around me. I was too caught up in my life, being the sheriff, and living in the fast lane. And, of course, there was the addiction. It smothered me, kept me from smelling, tasting, and experiencing the good things in life. It blinded me, too. It took being behind bars to open my eyes to what is really important, and so the clock lost all its meaning. My wife, Jennifer, recently offered to buy me a TAG Heuer watch. She said,

"You need it for work and meetings."

I appreciated the thought, but I kindly passed on her offer. Time has a whole new meaning to me now. When I was sheriff, and my kids were young, I showed up to their sporting events and important school activities. I was physically there, but I wasn't present. I never took photos because I was afraid they would capture an image of me that I didn't like. Photos of me in those days threatened to tell a story that I wasn't prepared to see with my own eyes. My addiction had a chokehold on me. I look back, and I realize that I missed out on so much.

These days, anytime I can snap a photo, I do! And I post it on social media! I'm not afraid to capture the "new me" because I am present and accounted for, not just physically but mentally, emotionally, and spiritually. I missed four years of my children's lives; that's time I can't get back. Today, I'm all in!

Addiction was a far worse sentence for me than going to prison. Those chains of dependence and compulsion shackled me, keeping me from being truly happy. It was one of the emptiest times in my life. I felt so alone, and I started asking myself, "What am I missing?"

I was chasing something that I could not see; I didn't know what it was. It was invisible. Today, I'm no longer chasing that thing, because there's nothing to chase. I have everything I could ever need—I've always had these things. I just didn't realize it. It took living in a six-by-nine cell, having lost everything under the sun, to understand the meaning of gratitude. I was a grown man, and the words "thank you" had never occurred to me. It took prison time, divorce, bankruptcy, and being away from my children for four years to make me feel thankful for what I had. I took so much for granted. I had been stripped down to a number. I was 692183.

I was nobody.

In my heart and mind, however, I was still a sheriff. I was still a husband, a father, and a son. But the truth is, those old identities had to die for me to live again. It was the only way the seeds of my transformation would take root. I had to lose everything, including my house, my car, and my possessions. But that didn't hurt nearly as much as losing people's trust in me. Life is about the relationships we build.

You can buy houses and cars, but you can't buy people, and, as cliché as it sounds, you can't buy love.

Back in 2015, when I was the sheriff, I hated looking in the mirror because I wasn't being honest with myself. I couldn't answer the hard questions, like what good am I? Where do I go from here? I didn't love myself. And how could I expect anyone else to love me if I didn't love me? I was an empty vessel of a human being—irredeemable, as far as I could tell—because without love, you've got nothing.

People today are so caught up in themselves, selling their souls for temporary internet fame and fortune. They're putting a monetary value on their happiness, forgetting that a Brinks truck will not be showing up at their funeral.

I can tell you from experience, friends and family will show up to celebrate your life, but only if you take responsibility for yourself and your relationships. In other words, be present and in the moment with the people you love.

That's where you'll find true happiness.

When I was Sheriff, I was so selfish. Addiction will do that. Plus, I was too proud to ask for help. Now, I go to therapy twice a month. These sessions empower me, and they can empower you too, because what you are doing is building a better version of who you already are. That's not weakness. That's strength, friend. If I hadn't asked for help, I wouldn't be writing this book right now, helping others through their journey with addiction.

Today, I can look at myself in the mirror and be proud of who I am. I may have bad moments in life, but I don't have bad days anymore. I can honestly say that I love myself, and that, in turn, has created a better, safer space for my relationships. I talk to my kids every day. My son initiates conversations. That would not have happened had I not loved myself enough to seek help. I am remarried to a beautiful woman. My parents are still in my life.

I can see now how my relationships reflect the love I have for myself and for the man I am becoming. I am no longer an empty vessel. I suspect God has always seen this in me. He's been there the whole time, waiting only for me to ask of Him.

In Matthew 7:7, it reads: "Ask, and it shall be given to you; seek, and you shall find; knock, and it shall be opened to you."[4]

I went to Catholic school all my life, and I never got to know God. It wasn't until I went to prison that I found God and gratitude— the two big Gs! That's sad to say, because He was always calling me. I just never heard Him, or if I did, I ignored Him. As time went on, however, I found myself praying to Him at night, asking that He protect my kids and my family.

I never really asked for my protection. I slept with a homemade shank in my cell; *that* was my protection. Most of us had some kind of piece, as it can get pretty dicey and dangerous in prison. You never know if somebody is going to attack you in your cell.

As I started having these conversations with God, I would ask myself: What am I going to do with my life when I get out of here? Will I work an average job? Will I do something meaningful with the time I have left? O or will I fall away like the changing leaves outside?

---

[4] *The Bible*, Matthew 7:7, King James Version

Of course, I had so many different things going through my head. I wondered, would I be stronger from this experience, able to make something of myself again? It was in those quiet moments with God that I decided to do and be something. I would take this experience (and my addiction) and use it for good. A lot of people would pander to me, telling me, "Oh, poor you! You're an addict."

No. God did not curse me with addiction. He gave me a gift. It is a blessing to be able to turn my mess into my message so that I can help others. I started day one in prison. I had to make that decision and stick to it. And, from day one, there were all kinds of temptations—drugs, alcohol, sex, etc. I could have had or done anything I wanted in there. However, I abstained, and it made me stronger. I adhered to the vision I had for my life.

People talk about their "dreams." I don't believe in dreams. Dreams are short-lived, something you have while taking a nap. Today, I have visions, a long-term goal, and it doesn't go away when I wake up. So much of my time was spent sitting and visualizing life after prison. I wanted my kids to be proud of me. I thought long and hard about the future, not the past. Therefore, I thought about becoming a speaker, sharing my story. Growing up, I was always vocal. I thought I could use my political prowess as a former sheriff, demonstrating that this disease does not discriminate. I mean, people's idea of addiction and mental health is so screwed up.

There is still a stigma.

So much so, for a long time, I struggled with forgiving myself. Until one day, my son, Dillon, who must have been nineteen or twenty years old at the time, looked at me and said, "Dad, it's over and done! Forgive yourself."

I am happy to say his words sunk in.

It wasn't easy. The Bible speaks a lot about forgiveness. Before prison, I was never a strong believer in God. There was a time I thought I was, but I wasn't. Now, I am. I have a tattoo on my arm of the Apostle Paul. He was kind of like me. He, too, spent four years in prison, and in those four years, he remained positive. It's where he wrote the book of Ephesians. Did you ever notice that Jesus used outlaws to move his story forward, men who sinned and struggled in life. In their walk with Him, he turned those bad men into superstars, and He will do the same for you and me—if we put our faith and trust in Him. He will transform our pain into our purpose. I could never have found my way out of solitary confinement and addiction without having faithfully endured the pain and discomfort in my walk with Him. It's been an uphill climb, but I know there's so much good to come of it. I've got a lot more to do, and if you are reading this book, so do you!

EPILOGUE
REDEMPTION

I t was just after Christmas, December 2016—I had just arrived at the Allen Correctional Institution in Lima, Ohio, where I would begin my four-year prison sentence. Upon entry, I was greeted by the unofficial rock bottom "welcoming committee," made up of several inmates eager to recruit me into their community. One inmate approached first, offering me opiates right off the bat.

"The first one is on me," he said. "The next one is on you."

I have to admit—I wasn't expecting five-star concierge service behind prison walls. But because my case was considered high-profile, these men knew my weakness from the start, and they weren't shy about bringing it up in conversation. This, being my first day as an inmate, would have been an opportune time for them to get me into the fold, as well as cause me to relapse. I suppose it would have been good for their business had I accepted the offer.

"There's not going to be a first or a next one," I replied.

I stood my ground that day and continued to serve my four-year sentence abstinent from any drugs or alcohol. Who would have thought that would have been an obstacle to overcome in lockup? It was clear that there would be a science to my survival as an inmate.

Because light always follows darkness, I was soon blessed to cross paths with another inmate named Black, a short, muscular, African-American man who had been incarcerated for over twenty years for participating in the Lucasville riots in April of 1993, when 450 prisoners revolted at the maximum-security Southern Ohio Correctional Facility in Lucasville. The standoff between rioting inmates, some of Ohio's most dangerous felons, and law enforcement lasted eleven days.

Black was a cornucopia of wisdom and truth, especially when it came to God and prison life. He was well-respected by the other inmates and always had a toothpick hanging out of his mouth, which made him appear 70's cool, especially when he'd use the phrase, "You dig?"

Black worked in the barber shop, cutting inmates' hair. I first met him in the barber's chair. I had accumulated a lot of hair during my long stay in administrative segregation (i.e., the hole), and he offered to shave it all off for me. I remember our conversation being extremely meaningful. It was as if we had known each other our whole lives. Black was a genuine guy, very well-spoken, and came across as well-educated. He was definitely not the type of character I expected to meet in prison, especially after some of the run-ins I had with criminals as a law enforcement officer.

In the days that followed that first shave, our discussions ranged from everyday survival and cooking to Black's deepening relationship with God. I learned a lot from him. I was grateful that he took me under his wing. Being new to prison life, I didn't have much going for me. I didn't even have money in "the books" (i.e., commissary account) for food, let alone snacks stored in my box underneath my bunk.

It's true what they say about the prison chow hall; it is unfit for human consumption, and other meal options are limited at best. However, in every prison, there is someone called the "Store Man." This is the cell-block's version of an entrepreneur, the guy who has extra items from the commissary that can be purchased, not with money, of course, but with other food items. And when it is time to pay him back, you can expect to owe double or even triple the following week. This is how the prison economic system works.

Anyway, Black took it upon himself to introduce me to the Store Man and used his name to front me the food items I would need to get started. Because of him, I had enough sustenance until money dropped into my commissary account. This act of kindness has stayed with me over the years, reminding me that you can't judge a person by their past. Black wasn't just a mentor to me. He was a good friend. And, unfortunately, his companionship was short-lived.

One day, he asked me to stop by his cell before the last lockdown of the night. I did as he asked, and for the last few minutes before the cell block went dark, we sat together on his bunk. Black told me that he was being transferred to another institution the following morning and that it was hard for him to say goodbye. It was hard for me, too. He expressed gratitude for our conversations and praised me for taking responsibility for my addiction and the crimes I had committed.

I was so grateful for this man's friendship and mentorship. Mostly, I was thankful that he was so generous in sharing his faith in Jesus with me. I can't help but think that he was ordained by God to give light to guys like me. Black and I shed a few tears together that night, vowing to reconnect one day. Then, he leaned in and said something I will never forget.

"If you think that you achieved something great by being the youngest Sheriff in Ohio, you haven't seen anything yet," he said. "When you are released from here, you'll find your true purpose, and you will help so many others find theirs, as long as you trust in God."

I let those words sink in.

Black and I exchanged a few letters, but we eventually lost touch. We've since reconnected, and as of today, he's served about thirty-seven years in prison. I have prayed for him over the years, and

I know for a fact he has prayed for me, too. He said he would. He's the kind of friend every man needs.

Well, Black, I'm writing this next big chapter in my life with you in mind. I'm naming it "Redemption." And I'm taking my Lord and Savior, Jesus Christ, along with me for the ride. I couldn't have done this without either one of you. Thank you for your friendship and belief in me. I'm a man on a mission to do for recovery what God (and your friendship) did for me—front hope for others and show up where I am needed most.

Pray for me, brother.

And Dad … as I travel down this road toward redemption, I am reminded of something you said on the day I was appointed Sheriff of Sandusky County. You said, "Kyle, you've got more balls than I ever had."

I don't know about that, Dad! But I do know that hearing those words from you meant everything to me. I've carried them with me all these years. They pulled me out of some really dark days. And so, I just want to end with this: "I love you, too, Dad!"

"Your past should never define you, only refine you."

—Kyle Overmyer

(Me pictured with UFC greats: Mark "the Hammer" Coleman & Wes Sims)

ACKNOWLEDGEMENTS
GRATITUDE LIST

T hank you, Deb Wingert, for giving me a place to live after my release from prison, when I had no place to call home. I will forever be grateful!

Thank you, Larry Bowman, for giving me a job frying chicken at Lee's Famous Recipe Chicken, when no one else would give me the opportunity of a second chance. The best chicken establishment ever!

Thank you, Nate Kehlmeier, for igniting my true purpose by giving me my first shot at working in the addiction and mental health space, helping others who are struggling.

Thank you, Bruce Joseph, for giving me my first speaking opportunity at the Exchange Club in Fremont, Ohio, where I began sharing my journey of addiction and shattering the stigma that goes with it.

Thank you, George Faerber and John Paull, for designing my book cover—the perfect way to illustrate my reclamation.

Thank you, Natalie June Reilly, for believing in me and for partnering with me in putting all my experiences, thoughts, words, and road to recovery on paper so that we might give hope to others. You never stopped encouraging me!

Lastly, and most importantly, I want to thank all those people who jumped ship and stopped believing in me when the going got tough. You all did me a favor, leaving room for those who know (and love) a good comeback story!

THE WEIGH-IN
WORDS FROM MY REAL-LIFE SUPPORT TEAM

"Even during his darkest chapter, Kyle's leadership potential and capacity to make a lasting impact were undeniable. As the youngest sheriff in Ohio, he once led from the front, and even in prison, I encouraged him to use that time for reflection and preparation for a greater purpose. I never doubted that he would transform his pain into purpose. Today, he is doing exactly that, using his experience to help others overcome addiction and reclaim their lives."

Corey D. Foster, M.A.,
Deputy Warden of Special Services

"Addiction doesn't discriminate! It doesn't care if you're male, female, black, white, rich, poor, or what your occupation is. No one chooses to become an opiate addict. Many times, it happens from prescription medications. The bottom line is, don't judge others until you have walked in their shoes. WE ALL NEED LOVE!!!"

Sheriff Stephen J. Levorchick,
Ottawa County—Ohio

"I didn't know Kyle before prison — I met him in the chapter where he chose redemption. His passion for helping others and breaking the stigma around addiction is what brought us together. Watching him turn his pain into purpose has been one of the greatest privileges of my life. I am endlessly proud to be his wife."

Jennifer Overmyer,
Kyle's Wife & Best Friend

"Kyle Overmyer's memoir is a rare look at the fall and redemption of a disgraced country sheriff. It's a brutally honest story about power, addiction, accountability—and the hard road back."

Matthew Cox,
Author of *Shark in the Housing Pool*

"Kyle's journey proves that mistakes may shape your story, but they never have to define the ending."

Orville O. Greene,
Drug Enforcement Administration
Special Agent in Charge (Retired)

"This is the true story of a man who lost his badge, his freedom, and his identity—only to discover the deeper purpose God had for him. From Power to Prison to Purpose Reborn reminds us that our worst failures can become the birthplace of our greatest calling."

Harvey Hook,
Author of *The Power of an Ordinary Life*

"Former Sandusky County, Ohio Sheriff Kyle Overmyer once upheld the law — until addiction brought him down. Redemption brought him back. His story is not just about a fall from power—it's about the courage to rise again with humility, faith, and a mission to serve. Where many would see only failure, Kyle chose reflection, accountability, and transformation. Today, he stands as proof that redemption is real, that purpose can be born from pain, and that the measure of a person is not how far they fall, but how faithfully they rise to help others along the way."

Haraz N. Ghanbari,
Ohio State Representative

Kyle Overmyer is the co-founder of KO Addiction, LLC and a nationally recognized advocate for mental health and addiction recovery. Once Ohio's youngest sheriff-elect, his life took a profound turn after his own battle with opioid addiction. His path through law enforcement, legal troubles, and recovery now fuels his mission to empower others facing similar struggles.

Today, Overmyer challenges stigma and inspires change, championing resilience, recovery, and mental wellness. He holds an associate degree in police science from Terra State Community College and a bachelor's degree in business administration from Tiffin University. A Certified Event Interventionist, he helps individuals navigate the system to access the quality of care they deserve. He serves on the board of One Brother One Sister, supporting first responders and military veterans, and is a governor-appointed board member of the Ohio Department of Rehabilitation & Correction Reentry Coalition.

Natalie June Reilly is a writer and editor known for her heartfelt storytelling, sharp editorial eye, and ability to bring depth, clarity, and humanity to every project she touches. With a passion for crafting narratives that resonate, she has built a career over the last 19 years helping individuals, organizations, and brands communicate with authenticity and impact.

From Fortune 100 companies to former NBA basketball players to self-made millionaires to law enforcement officers to mothers of fallen police officers to military spouses to combat veterans, Natalie approaches every story with curiosity and care, believing that the right words can inspire connection, hope, and healing. When she's not polishing sentences or developing meaningful narratives, you'll find her championing stories of resilience, purpose, and the everyday heroic moments that make us human.

WORK CITED

1. *The Bible*, Isaiah 41:10 New International Version

2. Seewer, John, "Mysterious cases of cancer in Ohio children puzzle parents and investigators," Lubbock Avalanche-Journal, December 30, 2010, Clyde, Ohio

3. *The Bible*, Philippians 4:19 English Standard Version

4. *The Bible*, Matthew 7:7, King James Version